Real Life F

Real Life Rev

A clergy survival guide

Martin Poole

CANTERBURY
PRESS

© Martin Poole 2025

Published in 2025 by Canterbury Press
Editorial office
3rd Floor, Invicta House,
110 Golden Lane,
London EC1Y 0TG, UK
www.canterburypress.co.uk

Canterbury Press is an imprint of Hymns Ancient & Modern Ltd
(a registered charity)

Hymns Ancient & Modern® is a registered trademark of
Hymns Ancient & Modern Ltd
13A Hellesdon Park Road, Norwich,
Norfolk NR6 5DR, UK

All rights reserved. No part of this publication may be reproduced,
stored in a retrieval system, or transmitted,
in any form or by any means, electronic, mechanical,
photocopying or otherwise, without the prior permission of
the publisher, Canterbury Press.

Martin Poole asserted his right under the Copyright, Designs and
Patents Act 1988 to be identified as the Author of this Work

British Library Cataloguing in Publication data

A catalogue record for this book is available
from the British Library

ISBN: 978 1 78622 587 0

EU GPSR Authorised Representative
LOGOS EUROPE, 9 rue Nicolas Poussin, 17000, LA ROCHELLE, France
E-mail: Contact@logoseurope.eu

Typeset by Regent Typesetting
Printed and bound by
CPI Group (UK) Ltd

Contents

Acknowledgements — vii
Foreword — ix

Introduction — xi

1 Give Us a Job — 1
2 Things May Not Be Quite as They Seem — 14
3 We All Fall Down — 21
4 We All Build Up — 31
5 The Joy of Sex in Church — 41
6 Food, Waste and Compost — 53
7 Music as Balm to the Soul — 65
8 Church and Community — 74
9 Church as a Refuge — 86
10 Doorstep Discoveries — 96
11 Religion and Politics — 107
12 Serving God and Mammon — 115
13 Happily Ever After — 123

Acknowledgements

With thanks to my wife and her enthusiasm for punctuation and to the wonderful people of St Luke's Prestonville who continue to support my attempts to serve them.

Foreword

by Bishop Rose Hudson-Wilkin

For the world outside looking in on the church, it is often thought that Sunday is the main day of work. *Real Life Rev* challenges this long-held perception, and from the very beginning we are in no doubt that ministry is an all-consuming adventure, and certainly not restricted to Sundays. For the many who think of Sundays as being a 'shop window', Martin, our 'real life Rev', confidently shares his conviction borne from experience, that 'Monday to Saturday is our shop window, the place where people get to experience the love of God in the social welfare projects we provide, and Sunday mornings should be a kind of staff meeting where all the shop workers gather to be refreshed and inspired for the work of the week.'

Real Life Rev is a resource full of ideas to explore, or indeed not explore, the way someone else has approached impossible tasks. It should be on the reading list for all who entertain thoughts of ministry as it removes any rose-tinted spectacles view of it. It introduces the reader to the sometimes harsh reality of parish ministry, and to the joys of walking alongside others and seeing the difference made by the Spirit at work in their lives. It also opens up the kind of immaturity present within the body of Christ, which allows those professing faith to behave like spoilt children having a hissy fit, or throwing a tantrum, and walking out and not practising what it means to love and forgive.

The raw honesty of the book deeply challenges our empty words of praise that are ungrounded in the reality of what it means to be 'sent out in the power of the Spirit to live and work to the praise and glory of God'. Reading the book gives new meaning to Paul's advice to 'put on the whole armour of Christ', because very often church can be a real battleground where there are some who think God is speaking directly to them, and only they somehow know the heart and mind of God and, therefore, there is no stepping back, no pause to reflect and allow room for the Spirit to thrive.

I am reminded of the words of the hymn 'There's a wideness in God's mercy', where the writer tells us we make God's love too narrow by our own false limits and that we express strictness with a zeal that God himself would not own. The words of this hymn capture the reality that many are experiencing in the Church.

I would love to see theological colleges engage with the themes encountered in this book on the Church's mission and ministry: how best to encourage a thriving parish system, the inability to address issues around finance, and what it means to give generously to the work of the Church. The new obsession around 'resource church' is also discussed: who it is for and why it is only attributed to certain styles of being church, and what it means to be a church serving the needs of the community of which it is a part.

I am often asked why I remain with the Church and my answer is always, 'Because I know who called me.' Knowing Martin, the real life Rev, he has continued in the life of the Church because he too knows who has called him. He may not have spoken about kneeling in prayer before and after every task, but when you meet Martin you will always see a joy that can only come from being fed by connection to the 'true vine'.

The Rt Revd Rose Hudson-Wilkin
Bishop of Dover

Introduction

How do you become a vicar? This question presupposes a couple of others such as what is a vicar, and why would anyone want to become one? These are both questions that this book seeks to explore, along with a 'warts and all' description of all the joys and troubles that I have experienced in following this path, which is not a job but a lifelong calling.

For me it began in my mid-teens. That's when I became a Christian and quickly developed an adolescent fervour for everything to do with faith, fuelled by involvement in a church going through charismatic renewal and a girlfriend similarly passionate about God. As the only young person in the church and someone who happened to be able to play the guitar, I found myself involved in leading worship after the choir and organist walked out in protest at these new-fangled services, and my self-important confidence naturally led to me thinking about becoming a church leader.

Then I went off to university and thoughts of ministry, and to a certain extent God, took a back seat to the pleasures of student life. Parties, Student Union gigs, the university drama society and occasionally studying for my science degree while taking on various casual jobs to try to address my growing overdraft – all distracted me somewhat from the religious life. It wasn't until my degree was over that my thoughts turned to the next stage of my life and the call of the church once more raised its head.

I managed to get accepted on a one-year church volunteering scheme and found myself placed in a church in the heart of Everton, Liverpool, with a brief to help out in any way that I could. Naturally, as a young person I was asked to focus on the young people, but I was also tasked with driving the church minibus to bring old people to church on Sundays as well as ferrying them around to various midweek groups. My time was filled playing football with the kids of dockers families and being taken to watch Liverpool at Anfield by their dads, sitting having cups of tea with rather smelly, lonely old men, and singing choruses with groups of mums who'd just had babies at the local children's hospital. On Sundays I helped to lead worship while watching the occasional brick bounce off the high-level bulletproof windows of the modern-style church – and learning about Orange lodges, Freemasons and the importance of setting the burglar alarm in the vicarage during the evening service on Sundays.

At the same time I made enquiries in my hometown of Salisbury about the process of going forward for ordination. These days the discernment process, as it's known in the Church of England, is quite a rigorous undertaking of study and discussion with a mentor, which takes at least two years and quite a lot of soul searching and academic work. My process was much simpler. I had a meeting with the Diocesan Director of Ordinands who then arranged for me to meet the bishop. They both seemed happy, and so sent me on a three-day selection conference at a retreat house in Chester. I thoroughly enjoyed my first ever experience of a retreat, although as an extrovert I found the silence at various parts of the day a little hard to maintain. The days were filled with one-on-one interviews with various members of a selection panel, some group discussions, one of which I was asked to lead, and a few set tasks.

My inexperience was shown up very quickly when I was asked what theological books I had read. The best I could manage was C. S. Lewis (by which I meant *The Lion the Witch and the Wardrobe*, not one of his more theological books) to which the interviewer asked: 'So you like apologetics?' My response was: 'If you say so!' He commented that I didn't seem to know much theology and I agreed and suggested that he approve me for ordination so that I could go to theological college to remedy that!

INTRODUCTION

Not everyone enjoyed the conference, and I remember that the very thin walls of my monk's cell of a room allowed me to hear the person in the next bedroom crying most nights, and I subsequently heard that he did not get recommended. Somehow I did get through and received a cautious letter from the bishop confirming this, along with a warning that I pay heed to the unusual advice from the selectors, to make sure I studied some theology during my training.

Taking this on board I began the task of touring around theological colleges, focusing on those I knew to be evangelical, as potential homes for my next three years of academic study. The visits included a long discussion about a girlfriend with one theological college principal, who later became Archbishop of Canterbury; taking tea with a student at another college, which consisted of a bunch of twigs in a fine bone china cup with no handle; and going to the pub with an old friend who was a year ahead of me at another college, which needless to say became the one I chose.

This was followed by three years of residential training at college (a luxury these days when most ordinands train from home in ecclesiastical versions of the Open University). I broke my leg in a motorbike accident and missed my first-year exams, nearly got thrown out of college for screening *The Life of Brian*, organized a mini music festival in the grounds of the college, and helped to run a street theatre company.

This latter activity led to increased involvement in performing, including acting in two musical versions of the Easter story (my only line in one being 'Pah! Look at you now!'). I took a night class in acting at the local city college, and a summer school with an old battleaxe of the theatre who spoke and behaved like Dame Edith Evans in *The Importance of Being Earnest*. These experiences helped with the practical placements organized by the college, which included a weekly Sunday morning slot on BBC local radio and a month on manoeuvres with the army in Germany. All this playing around with acting was much more rewarding than learning New Testament Greek (which I flunked). But following the advice from the bishop I did engage in the deeper realms of theology, reading Nietzsche, Hume and Wittgenstein who all thought God was too ineffable to be studied or even talked about. This led me back to the importance of symbolism and symbolic action, particularly in relation to the Eucharist, and fuelled my urge to perform even more.

Theological college was a revelation to me as it opened my eyes to the depth and variety of academic thought about faith while also allowing me to pursue my interest in creative arts and especially theatre. During my three years of study for the priesthood I became more and more convinced that God was calling me to something slightly different from what I was seeing most vicars doing, and that maybe my talents as an extrovert and an artist were better suited to a different kind of ministry. This was encouraged by various people I knew who worked in theatre, most notably friends in Riding Lights Theatre Company in York and the Arts Centre Group in London.

All of this combined with a strong passion for mission ended up with a decision not to be ordained at the end of my three years but to try and get into drama school. Consequently, I left theological college after completing my studies but instead of becoming a curate and starting work in a parish, I headed off to drama school.

This change in direction wasn't met with universal approval, and some of those church folk who had nurtured and supported me in my calling were understandably upset with me, especially when I wrote to them asking if they'd be prepared to stump up £10 a month for a year to help me fund yet another year as a student. Auditions for drama school led to me being awarded a scholarship for a one-year postgraduate diploma at Guildford School of Acting, and enough generous souls agreed to support me financially to take up the place to 'learn my craft' as they say in the business.

There then followed five years of working as an actor, during which time I was fortunate to get married and found myself in South London involved with our local parish and the vicar, a certain Revd Dr John Sentamu, who in later life went on to become Archbishop of York. It was John who suggested that I

INTRODUCTION

should revisit my former calling and, since I had done the training, get ordained and help him out in the parish, and so I became a deacon in Southwark Cathedral in 1987 and a priest in 1988.

Shortly after being ordained, I was assigned a local bishop as my mentor because I was unable to do the regular post-ordination training (or potty training as we called it), and he told me that being called to be a priest, especially in my case, was a calling to be the person God created me to be rather than asking me to slot into a particular job description. I have carried that advice with me ever since and it has been my guiding light through a rather unusual path of ministry. This goes against the current businessification of church, where everyone has a job description (or as the Church describes it, a 'Statement of Particulars') and is expected to deliver on objectives and have a strategy for their parish.

After being ordained I worked as much as I could as an actor, while relying on my wife's income as an administrator to keep a roof over our heads and food on the table. My ministry consisted of helping out at the church on Sundays and coming up with crazy pieces of semi-religious street theatre with a group of willing and enthusiastic friends. My vicar and the congregation of the church were extraordinarily accepting of my mad ideas, and let me experiment with our services on occasion, while also giving me a great grounding in the basics of Church of England liturgy and worship. Being inspired by the National Theatre's promenade staging of *The Mysteries*, I devised a Palm Sunday promenade service. I thought it would help us all to step into the shoes of the crowds as Jesus entered Jerusalem, and so I removed all the chairs from the school hall that we were using for our Sunday services and had the whole congregation follow me to different corners of the room for different parts of the service. I thought it was a great success, and it wasn't until the following year, when I asked if we could repeat the idea, that I discovered that there had been a number of complaints about my Palm Sunday innovation and requests never to do it again.

My working life blossomed as I discovered a talent for sourcing and managing complex television branding projects, working for various agencies including the BBC and a major Hollywood design and production company, all the while continuing to keep my calling bubbling away on Sundays. As a family we relocated to the South coast for a better quality of life for our children and because we wanted to be by the sea. I set up my own consulting business and developed a raft of international clients who kept me busy and were happy to fly me around the world delivering my advice and expertise on their brand values and how to express these with design and graphics. This work bled into my faith life as I sought to bring some of the creativity and symbolism that had so inspired me to think of the priesthood in the first place into my practice as a non-stipendiary minister. It was in this space that the call of God to become a parish priest got louder and louder.

This is the story of where that call has taken me, what that call looks like in daily life, and the joys and calamities that are part of the life of a parish priest.

1

Give Us a Job

Some people might think that being a priest is a job like any other, some might even think of it as a career, although very few priests I know are interested in career progression or climbing up some kind of ecclesiastical ladder. Being a priest is a calling, a vocation (from the latin *vocare* to call or be summoned) rather than a job. It was finding myself without a church to help out at and getting involved with art projects that finally drew me away from an actual job to consider parish ministry. I'd spent a couple of years setting up an arts collective called Beyond, and developing all sorts of public art projects such as the world's first Beach Hut Advent Calendar (you can read about this in *Church Beyond Walls*)[1] while pursuing a career as a branding and promotion consultant for TV companies. I found myself spending more and more time working on crazy art events that expressed something about God, and less and less time working on my consulting business and tracking down new clients to keep that afloat.

I began to wonder if God was calling me away from TV work to become a full-time priest, and I secretly began to pray about this before eventually saying something to my wife. Oddly, I didn't think of it in terms of giving up a lucrative international consulting career, but as finally returning to something I'd first felt as a teenager, fresh to Christian faith. Almost as soon as I'd mentioned this to my wife, we heard through the grapevine that a vicar in central Brighton had announced his intention to move on. We had been to the church once or twice, which had a modern interior complete with lots of audio-visual tech and quite a lively style of worship. This was unusual in Brighton, which was dominated at the time by very traditional Anglican churches, due to a quirk of late Victorian history and the influence of a wealthy family keen on reintroducing Roman Catholic tradition into the Church of England and building a number of churches to exemplify that.

We visited the church one Sunday and the feeling that this might be the right place for us began to grow. So I wrote to the Bishop of Chichester asking if I might be considered for the post once it became vacant. It's remarkable how things have changed in the administration of church vacancies since 2010. I already had experience of how jobs for priests could be handed out at the whim of a bishop in a way that would be regarded as unfair today, and I suppose by writing to the bishop I was taking advantage of that same practice. Nowadays church vacancies are almost always advertised in the *Church Times*, or appear on lists created by various church organizations, and are added to an online jobs portal available to all clergy who are looking to move. The process of applying and being interviewed and appointed to the role of vicar, rector or associate priest, is mostly open and transparent, but can also be quite rigorous and time consuming, sometimes involving day-long interviews, trial sermons and strategy presentations at the same time as other potential candidates, with all the stress and pressure that entails.

Back in 2009 all I did was write to the bishop who replied that he thought it sounded like a good idea and that I should talk to the Archdeacon to make arrangements. Contacting him resulted in a lunch date with the two churchwardens, who both seemed very much on the same page as me as we talked about reading books by writers such Brian McLaren and Dave Tomlinson. And they were in favour of the ordination of women, which was one of the topics that every priest was asked about at the time. They were both enthusiastic about me becoming their vicar on the basis of this minimal contact, and so we proceeded to a formal interview which included the Archdeacon and a representative of the patrons of the church. This all went very well and I was informed that I could go ahead and take up the job.

Church patronage is an archaic and old-fashioned historical system which has been in place since before the reformation, where an institution or individual is the patron of a particular church and therefore has the right to be involved in the appointment of a vicar. In the past these patronages were bought and sold by organizations who wanted to ensure a particular church tradition was maintained, but they are also sometimes owned by individuals and bishops who wish to have an influence on churchmanship. In recent years this system has come into play as the Church of England has discussed the ordination of women as priests and bishops, and as the Church has wrestled with the issue of sexuality and the confirmation of long-term same-sex partnerships. Some organizations that hold patronages have sought to ensure that priests are appointed who will 'hold the line' on women in leadership or the blessing of civil partnerships. In 2009, having basically already agreed to take the post after shaking hands with the churchwardens, I then went through the formality of an interview with the patron of St Luke's, who represented a large evangelical organization. It was a very pleasant meeting and the only question I remember the patron asking was about my views on the ordination of women which I whole heartedly supported. Fortunately, he didn't ask me about my views on homosexuality as that might well have ruled me out as far as they were concerned.

So, the deal was done and we could move on to the practicalities of starting work. The first thing to deal with was housing. Vicars are expected to live in the vicarage which goes along with the post and is seen as part of their compensation. The vicarage was an enormous, detached Edwardian house right next to the church. Walking in we discovered a long, high-ceilinged lounge coated in dingy green woodchip wallpaper. Down the centre of the room were a couple of trestle tables and 1980s steel and foam church chairs in a dull shade of blue. Upstairs, one of the seven large bedrooms was being used as a den for a youth group and was full of bean bags and had graffiti on the walls. Every piece of woodwork in the house looked as though a dog had tried to chew through it, somehow even including the lintels. The toilets were all absolutely black and two of the bedrooms at the top of the house had enormous patches of damp on the ceiling and chimney breast.

I thought that was it, the deal would have to be called off as my wife would never want to live in this dilapidated, beaten-up house being used as a surrogate church hall. Fortunately, she had much more vision than me, could see some potential in the house and was surprisingly upbeat about the prospect of remodelling it. Fortunately, we had three months before I was due to start work and so we began the process of negotiating with the diocese to sort this out.

Property ownership is a quirky business in the Church of England, featuring an odd mix of ancient tradition and modern property management. In the old days a vicar took possession of the church building when he took up the job; he was literally given the freehold of the building and became the owner. Not so with vicarages that remained part of the estate of the diocese, and so the fabric of the house is maintained by the diocese but the decoration and internal styling of it is down to the PCC of the church. Clearly manky toilets, distressed doorframes and damp ceilings were the responsibility of the diocese but we also wanted to turn the woodchipped meeting room/lounge into a kitchen/diner and the whole place would need redecorating, something the PCC could not afford.

After a fair bit of negotiation, we managed to persuade the diocese that this needed to be addressed, and various contractors began work instructed either by us or the diocese. Alongside this major work, some congregation members offered to help with the decoration, and so we arranged some work parties with willing church folk stripping woodchip off the walls and helping to do the easier decorating tasks while professionals did wallpapering and sanding and varnishing some of the rooms. We had some difficulty with deliveries as it turned out that the vicarage was located on a long road that went from Brighton through Hove, Portslade and Southwick with the house numbers being duplicated in each of these neighbourhoods. Some of our kitchen ended up being delivered to the same number house in Hove and we were constantly having to make sure deliveries referenced our postcode, not just the number.

In the middle of all this manual labour, I decided I needed to do something spiritual to mark this change in my life. I had long harboured the desire to have a tattoo but never had a good enough reason for getting one or much of an idea of what design I wanted. This felt like an opportunity to satisfy this desire and gave me an excuse for anyone who might think it was inappropriate or immature. I had heard about a tradition in the Coptic church of having a small tattoo on your wrist when you are baptized, a tradition that extends to children as well as adults. I'd also seen that in some circumstances this was just a series of five small dots in a cross shape as an identification mark for Christians in cultures where Christianity was forbidden. I decided this would legitimize adorning my body and that in a small way I was identifying with those who were persecuted for their faith.

I chose a design based on the Canterbury Cross which I was told was the form of an ancient brooch found under Canterbury Cathedral. It's an image full of meaning as it is a cross made from a broken circle representing our broken world, it contains four triangles symbolizing the trinity and of course is a cross reminding us of Jesus' crucifixion. I drew a version of this to size to fit the inside of my wrist and headed out to a local tattoo parlour for some pain. I think I had a trainee tattooist that day because it seemed to take a long time and there was a lot of examining of the design and drawing things on my wrist followed by vigorous scratching back and forth with the tattoo gun and a lot of ink splurging around. I'd asked for this to be on the inside of my right wrist which is quite a sensitive place for a procedure like this, and the hour it took to draw seemed much longer as I gritted my teeth and looked the other way. Eventually it was complete and the ink and blood were wiped away to reveal my tattoo, not as crisp or clear as I had hoped, with fuzzy lines and wonky curves and the whole thing slightly askew. But there wasn't much I could do about it, you can't erase a tattoo and I wasn't about to go through more hours of pain to try and adjust it. I live with this tattoo every day and have grown to love its imperfection as a symbol of my imperfect ministry and as a sign of God's love for all every time I raise my hand in blessing.

While all this was going on, I was also working with the church and the diocese on the format of the licensing service. The liturgy for this is fixed but there is scope to personalize the service with the choice of readings and songs. I was given a template for the service, and already knew from the parish profile that there was a part-time worship leader who would be selecting songs for the service, but I had some very clear opinions about this myself and there were certain themes for some songs which had to fit with the liturgy. I was already quite experienced in stretching the Anglican framework to suit a more contemporary mindset, and so a negotiation began between me, the worship leader, a friend who was a well-known Christian song writer, and the diocese about the musical content.

Those discussions went very well, and very quickly we had a set of approved songs, but there was a bigger issue that I needed to deal with before we could say that everything was settled. The church had a very simple layout with a rectangular main space facing a slightly raised chancel, which had a curved back wall or apse that was reminiscent of the side chapels in cathedrals. This space was packed full of worship band equipment, because clearly this was where the musicians 'performed'. I had two problems with this.

Firstly, there was the question of where to seat the Archdeacon, who expected to be in a position of respect as the most important person in the room, conveniently ignoring Jesus' many sayings about the first being last, the need for servant leadership and that people shouldn't think too highly of themselves by sitting in a place of honour. The second problem was that this arrangement meant that the focus for the congregation was on the musicians when I thought it ought to be on God. It was true that there was a large wooden cross hanging in the middle of the arch framing the chancel, but all the 'action' during a service was focused on the band as if this was some sort of music gig. There can be a tendency in some churches to worship the worship rather than God. This applies to all traditions and forms of liturgy and isn't confined to evangelical churches with worship leaders and bands. It can also be true of more traditional catholic-style worship when the choir and organist and the performance of the liturgy can also become the congregational focus.

I decided to tackle these two problems together and to insist that the band be moved off to one side as we needed to seat the Archdeacon in the chancel. There was a third complication as the service included me being 'placed in my stall'. A stall is the prayer desk and seat in most churches from which the priest conducts the service, but this church didn't have a stall (although a few years later I discovered two stalls in the church cellar). I was uncomfortable with having a specially exalted place to sit, so I managed to persuade the Archdeacon that it was OK for me to be placed in an ordinary seat alongside my family in the congregation. This felt like the kind of servant leadership that I hoped to exhibit in my ministry in this place.

I had, and still have, a very strong sense of my unworthiness for ministry and that this calling is about service as modelled by Jesus when he got down on his knees at the Last Supper and washed the feet of the disciples. As a teenager, new to faith, I had come across the book of Hebrews, which has a lot to say about priesthood and describes Jesus as our great high priest. So I chose some verses from Hebrews as the first reading:

> *We have a great high priest, who has gone into heaven, and he is Jesus the Son of God. That is why we must hold on to what we have said about him. Jesus understands every weakness of ours, because he was tempted in every way that we are. But he did not sin! So whenever we are in need, we should come bravely before the throne of our merciful God. There we will be treated with undeserved kindness, and we will find help.*
>
> *Every high priest is appointed to help others by offering gifts and sacrifices to God because of their sins. Such a high priest can be kind to people who do not know what is right and who do wrong. They know how to share in the suffering of others because they themselves are weak. Because they are weak, they*

must make sacrifices to God for the wrong things they have done, just as they do for the people. No one chooses to be a high priest. But God calls them, just as he called Aaron.
Hebrews 4.14—5.4 (Contemporary English Version)

I am as flawed a human being as anyone else, and wearing a clerical collar does not make me a better person. I find great comfort in the idea that Jesus understands what it's like to be a human being and that priests can only minister to those in their care because they understand human frailty. I hope I never get so full of myself that I forget that I too am imperfect and in need of God's grace and forgiveness.

At the front of the service sheet, I suggested that people might like to use the time while they waited for the service to start to pray for me, my family and the parish. I included a prayer that they could use:

Lord God, maker and lover and enlivener of all, look with mercy on all the people of this place and especially Martin and his family. So draw their hearts to you that your heart may live in them, and living in them, bring peace to the surrounding community and the world; through Jesus Christ the Prince of Peace. Amen.

Looking back on this prayer I'm surprised by how prescient, but at the same time contradictory, it was. In the years to come there were certainly many times when mercy was needed both for me and all the people of this place, and I'm afraid that following what I believed to be God's heart led to quite a lot of discord rather than peace.

One of the odd things about a licensing service is that the person being licensed doesn't normally get to say anything except to read the declarations and oaths. Any personal comments are restricted to the end of the service when they are asked to give the notices. I often say that notices are one of the hallmarks of an Anglican church, regarded by some as the most important part of the service. Since I hadn't been able to add any words of my own to the service up to that point, I decided that this was my opportunity to break with tradition, some would say starting where I meant to go on. I asked the congregation to sit down as I was going to be some time, because 22 years had passed since being ordained as a priest and 30 years since being selected for training and there were plenty of people I needed to thank as I made that journey.

It took 15 minutes to tell some of the stories of the years it had taken for me to eventually realize my calling as a parish priest. To thank those who had been patient with me every time I changed my mind, those who had supported me financially, those who had helped me spiritually and of course my family members who had made a considerable sacrifice as they accompanied me on this transition from a proper job to being a vicar. At the end of the longest notices ever uttered in a Church of England service I announced that we would hold a service of Holy Communion at 10.30am on Sunday. I then handed back to the Archdeacon who was getting a bit impatient with this upstart vicar and wondering whether he'd made the right decision to appoint me.

Much of this was symbolized by a beautiful gift given to me by my wife just before the licensing service. Priestly robes include a stole which is a kind of scarf that sits around the back of the neck with the two ends hanging down the front of the person to the knees or thereabouts. The origin of the stole is not entirely clear. It could be a reference to prayer shawls, or the towel that Jesus wrapped around himself to wash the disciples' feet, or it could simply be a symbolic version of a scarf designed to keep the priest warm in cold churches. My wife had commissioned a textile artist friend to create a stole for me to mark the occasion and the two ends featured a gorgeous collage of different coloured scraps of material with embroidery and stitching creating patterns and designs. On one end of the stole were five different sized sailing boats riding on a colourful sea of gauze and felt. This represented my family, with myself, my wife and our three children all sailing along on the ocean of God's love. The other end showed three beach huts as a reminder of the Father, the Son and the

Holy Spirit and a nod towards my most successful combination of art, creativity and mission in the Beach Hut Advent Calendar. It was a beautiful gift and I treasure it to this day and wear it whenever I can.

I got another chance to go through the whole rigmarole again three years later because this first time I was only licensed as priest-in-charge. The status of appointment as the minister of a church is a complicated process, which has changed since the days when a priest was appointed as vicar or rector, was handed the freehold of the church and left to get on with it. Now there are a variety of different types of appointment that are all related to what's called Common Tenure, which was introduced in January 2011. In 2010 I was appointed as priest-in-charge because the parish was theoretically under the possibility of a pastoral reorganization plan. This was a series of proposals to adjust some of the parishes in Brighton, combining some and closing others to make a more rational ecosystem of churches across the city. While these proposals hung in the air, any parish subject to possible change was 'suspended' and therefore could only appoint a priest on a temporary basis. In reality these reorganization proposals had not been acted on for years and would likely never happen but the upshot was that my 'employment' was a little precarious, as was the future of the parish church.

A note about 'employment' of priests. We are not employed by anyone temporal but serve at the pleasure of the creator of the universe. As it would be impossible to take God to an employment tribunal if there was any dispute about work practices or conditions of employment, priests do not have employment contracts; we are deemed to be 'post holders' which gives us some rights akin to employment such as sick pay, entitlement to holidays, maternity or paternity leave etc. but stops short of being an employment contract. As part of this we agree a 'Statement of Particulars' which is the closest thing we have to a job description – which begs the question why don't we call it a job description, but the Church loves to have its own names for things that everyone else already has a title for. This is all quite recent and came into force in January 2011, just six months after I became the priest-in-charge looking after St Luke's Prestonville.

I became aware of this insecurity due to a little administrative reorganization in our deanery, especially as I had just been elected to the Diocesan Mission and Pastoral Committee, which turned out not to be my understanding of mission or pastoral work but was solely about the organization of parishes and their churches and appointment of clergy. I thought that St Luke's deserved to have its place in the church landscape of Brighton confirmed and so applied to have the suspension of the living removed. This was agreed fairly swiftly, along with the lifting of the suspension of some other parishes who were all theoretically under the same reorganization plan, and I heard that I could now be licensed as vicar rather than just priest-in-charge.

This second licensing was going to be a much grander affair than the first because I managed to find a date when the bishop could come as well as the Archdeacon and Rural Dean. I still wanted the overall theme to be about service, so we stayed with the reading from Hebrews for this service, but the Gospel reading was the story of Jesus washing the disciples' feet. I quickly became aware of my lack of Church knowledge when talking to the Archdeacon about the date and how pleased he was that it was on the festival of 'Pip and Jim'. This turned out to be the colloquial term for the day the church remembers the disciples Philip and James and he wanted to point out that we should wear red stoles but I wasn't about to sideline the beautiful stole commissioned by my wife. At the rehearsal the day before I was further thrown when he asked where we kept our corporals. I wondered if I'd missed some kind of military connection that we should have established with the local army barracks and where we would put any soldiers who did turn up. It turns out the corporal is the linen cloth placed on the table underneath the chalice and paten so as to catch any stray crumbs and therefore save the body of Christ from inappropriate treatment. Being the kind of church that is fairly relaxed about our practice at communion we were a bit challenged in the linen department but fortunately the Archdeacon said he would bring some.

This time I was delighted to discover that we were going to enact some real, physical symbolic acts which were omitted from my licensing as priest-in-charge.

As a sign that I was now the vicar, the churchwarden and Archdeacon led me to the door of the church and placed my hand upon the key in the lock saying:

> *I induct you into the real, actual and corporal possession of the Vicarage and Parish Church of St Luke Prestonville with all the rights, members and appurtenances thereunto belonging.*

I then got to lock and unlock the door before moving to the other end of the church and ringing the single bell that we have at St Luke's. The usual instructions were then for the incumbent to be conducted to their stall and we maintained the ritual from the first licensing and I took my seat in the front row beside my family. It was comforting to hear the Archdeacon then pronounce:

> *The Lord preserve your going out and your coming in, from this time forth for evermore.*

There has certainly been a lot of going out and coming in since then and it's good to be reminded of the prayer that was said over me at the beginning of that service:

> *Almighty and everlasting God,*
> *by whom all virtues are given and perfected,*
> *give your grace, we pray you, to your servant, Martin,*
> *that he may worthily fulfil the charge now to be committed*
>   *to him.*
> *Give him vision, courage and love;*
> *that, following in the steps of Jesus Christ,*
> *he may lead your people to serve your kingdom and to*
>   *share its joy;*
> *through our Lord Jesus Christ, your Son,*

*who lives and reigns with you and the Holy Spirit, God, for
ever and ever.
Amen.*

Note

1 Martin Poole, *Church Beyond Walls: Christian Spirituality at Large*, Canterbury Press, 2023.

2

Things May Not Be Quite as They Seem

How do you tell what a church is like? You might be able to infer something of the character of a church by the architecture and decor but that ignores the fact that a church is the people not the building. Of course, it's true that the people dictate the appearance of the church to a certain extent but often the building is constrained by its history and what goes on inside it may be very different. Many of our churches were built in the Victorian era and reflect the values and culture of that time, values and practices which have shifted massively since then. Also, the styling of a church doesn't necessarily give you a clue to the theological make-up of its congregation. A church that is full of ornamentation, icons and stained glass may tell you something about its preferred liturgical style but doesn't say anything about its political outlook, attitude to women, same-sex relationships or even certain tenets of doctrine. Theological opinion can change much more rapidly than church architecture, but the other side of that coin is that personal attitudes can become fixed and immovable even when a church building has been adapted and modernized.

My first impressions of St Luke's were dominated by the appearance of the building, which was a medium-sized Victorian brick building which felt quite spacious inside due to the removal of the pews in 2000, leaving a lovely flexible space with a red-tiled stone floor and steel-framed, foam-cushioned chairs which could be moved around at will, if you were strong enough to do it as they were quite heavy. A modern approach to worship was exemplified by the fixed video projectors and screens and a sophisticated sound system and computer setup. The colour scheme was a bit dubious as the walls were painted sky blue with yellow accents but to me this gave an indication that there was a colourful undertone to this place and the people who congregated there, hinting at a spirit of fun and a relaxed attitude that was unusual in an Anglican church. The chancel was piled high with all the paraphernalia of a modern worship band with amps, keyboards and a full drumkit behind plexiglass screens, which also gave an indication of what one could expect in Sunday worship.

On the north side of the church a café area had been created with aluminium tables and wicker chairs, separated off from the main worship space by a waist high garden fence straight out of a garden centre and so it had an odd rustic flavour. This meant that the seating for worship was confined to the main body of the church and everyone decamped to the café at the end of the service for refreshments served from a servery in the north-east corner. This was convenient as it was right next to a kitchen in what used to be the vestry, which was kitted out with second-hand kitchen units donated by a churchwarden, a large cooker and a fridge.

The second impression came from reading the parish profile. Every church in vacancy is encouraged to write a parish profile which describes something about the church ethos, has some facts and figures about the parish and sets out something of the vision of the church for the future. It usually also includes some sort of description of the kind of person the church would like as their next leader.

Reading the parish profile was very encouraging as it had a clear description of the vision and values of the church, something which I was pleased to see because my previous day job had been working as a brand consultant for TV companies and I had spent all of my working days discussing these kinds of things with my clients. It included some statements about being a forward-looking congregation, wanting to be open to a diverse range of people and treating all with generosity and compassion.

All of this echoed my view of church and felt like a good fit. Added to that there was a list of staff and volunteers that included a worship and student pastor, two part-time administrators and a range of volunteer leaders for various initiatives such as a toddler group, youth club and assisting with worship. All of this was backed up by good financial resources and a summary set of accounts that had a very healthy bottom line. This all looked a bit too good to be true – and I discovered later that it was.

The congregation was described as being unusually young for a Church of England church and included a lot of young families with children as well as a significant group of young people attending both a church study group and an open youth club. There was a section in the profile of 'desired characteristics of the next incumbent' which had been compiled following a survey of the congregation and included that the person should be a gifted preacher, teacher and pastor, experienced in managing staff and able to develop a relationship with the parish and impact local residents because Sunday attendance largely relied on people travelling in to the church from other parts of the city and beyond, with some people travelling 20 or 25 miles to attend church activities. My only personal experience of the congregation had been when visiting one Sunday to see what the worship was like and what I'd been told in my previous discussions with the churchwardens, I didn't expect there to be any problems as I looked forward to getting to work.

The discord began just three months after being licensed when a prominent member of the congregation asked to come and see me. I welcomed them into the vicarage with a cup of tea and a few pleasantries before settling down for what I thought would be a genial chat. The opening words after sitting down were 'Well vicar, we know God didn't give you the gift of preaching did he!' After that initial shock I was then told that the trouble with my preaching was that it was all just my opinion and the congregation didn't want my opinion, they wanted the truth!

I was tempted to respond with the famous line from Jack Nicholson in *A Few Good Men* and say 'you can't handle the truth' but I was too surprised to think of a clever answer like that on the spur of the moment and on reflection I'm not sure it would have gone down well anyway. What did follow was a 90-minute discussion on biblical truth, the inerrancy of Scripture, the true purpose of preaching and my many failings in understanding any of this. I decided to take the humble servant approach and listen carefully, occasionally asking questions or making gentle comments, determined not to get into an argument as that wouldn't have helped either of us and I was still new to being a vicar and thought that maybe this was the kind of thing that vicars had to listen to all the time. I now know that isn't the case!

There is a certain kind of evangelical confidence in belief that can be very judgemental of others and accusatory in tone, especially when speaking to those who they see as being in error. Despite Jesus' many exhortations not to judge others and to pay attention to the log in our own eye before we go around pointing out splinters in others, there is something about the Christian who is certain of their faith and the infallibility of their particular set of beliefs that can lead to condemnation of others who don't share those views. We seem to see more and more of that in the Church, especially in relation to the discussions that the Church of England has been having around sexuality and same-sex relationships. Inerrancy in Scripture has morphed into a form of inerrancy in doctrine which suggests that the holders of the true faith cannot possibly be wrong about anything and that anybody who doesn't hold the same set of beliefs as them is therefore a heretic. This then leads to shunning them and, in some cases, abuse which seems to me to be incredibly un-Christian.

This initial skirmish into the world of doctrinal disagreement began to escalate as time progressed and I began to be aware that there was a group within the congregation who were not my greatest fans and who were bolstered by their solidarity to start making their feelings known. I didn't mind people coming up to me after a service and letting me know that they disagreed with my sermon but it was a bit of a shock when some of them started to vocalize their disagreement quite loudly while I was still talking! In theory I am in favour of teaching in the church being a two-way process but shouting out your disagreement in the middle of a sermon is perhaps not the best way to express the unity of the church, especially if there are any visitors to our worship.

This concern about the theology of the vicar got a boost when I invited a friend who was a priest and author to come and talk about his new book. I gave him a little briefing about the disagreements that had begun to surface in the congregation and asked him to be mindful of that in his talk. He duly obliged and I felt he was a bit bland in his presentation and was very diplomatic during the Q&A at the end of the evening. He then sat down to sign copies of his book and a small queue of people formed to collect an autograph or to ask a question. The evening was drawing to a close and numbers were dwindling when one of the congregation approached him and asked if he believed that Jesus had died for his sins. He replied in a very offhand way, 'oh no', and went back to signing books, unaware that there was sudden silence from those who had heard the answer. The church cleared out pretty quickly after that and I was soon the only person left in church with the speaker. I had overheard this and was slightly concerned about his answer and quizzed him about it, to be told that he took the questioner to mean did he believe in substitutionary atonement (the idea that Jesus died in our place to satisfy God's anger at us for being sinners) and that wasn't a theory of the atonement that he subscribed to.

A few days passed and I received a letter, signed by a few members of the congregation including the person who had asked the question. They were outraged that I should have invited someone to speak at the church who didn't believe what they regarded to be one of the basic tenets of Christian faith and expressing concern that I was taking St Luke's away from an orthodox evangelical position. Not only was my friend clearly a heretic who didn't deserve to be a priest but I must share his views as I had been the person who had invited him to our church. I also discovered that he had been contacted directly by some attendees similarly concerned about his apostate position.

There followed a series of exchanges between myself, my friend and the letter writers, including passing on a portion of another book he had written explaining about different theories of atonement and outlining why the idea of a vengeful God didn't sit comfortably with him. The communication included a reassurance that he did believe that Jesus' crucifixion was an important part of our salvation and an offer to visit again to talk to the Parochial Church Council (PCC) about this whole issue. I felt that a discussion like this might just inflame the dissension and prolong the disagreement so let the discussion around this run its course until it ran out of steam. I began to realize that the kind of open questioning about details of faith and doctrine which I was so used to in my life as a Christian was not welcome to certain members of this congregation.

When I trained to be a priest my experience at theological college was that it was very good at getting me to look critically at my faith, my understanding of the Bible, my engagement with church and worship and all sorts of other aspects of being a follower of Jesus. For me this was a transformative experience which strengthened my faith in God and enriched my life as a Christian. I believe I share this with many who train for the priesthood, although of course there are always those who arrive at college so sure of their faith that nothing they learn there will change them. I cherish this critical reflection on what it means to be a Christian and I carry this with me into my ministry because I believe it's important to be authentic as we seek to lead and minister to those in our care. It puzzles me that so many of my colleagues who seemed to share this view at college then abandon it when they get into a parish and slip into an alliance with their congregation which doesn't question anything. Many congregations, especially at the evangelical end of the spectrum, do not want to question anything and see enquiry and exploration of ideas as antithetical to faith – even dangerous.

This was exemplified by a member of the congregation who told me that they had decided what they were going to believe 30 years ago when they became a Christian and they weren't going to change anything now. The fact that I was happy to preach a sermon that left questions hanging was extremely uncomfortable for some. They wanted to be told what to believe and how to behave and my open subjective approach didn't fit with that.

I sometimes wonder if people's personal faith is a bit like believing in Santa Claus: once you start asking questions about him you will eventually find out (spoiler alert) that he doesn't exist and all your Christmas dreams are shattered. For some, believing in God is a bit like that: once you start asking questions there is a chance that the whole house of cards might collapse and you find yourself without a faith to hold onto. For me faith is indelibly tied up with questioning and doubt, otherwise it's not faith. We talk about making a leap of faith, which implies that we don't quite know where that launching out is going to take us, that's what's so exciting about having faith in Jesus Christ and why it takes an element of trust. I may be naive in thinking that God will hold on to me no matter what or where I choose to go with my life, but that is essential to my journey as a follower of Jesus, and my understanding of that journey is constantly changing and being enriched. I heartily recommend asking questions as part of our Christian practice.

Equally I understand that as a priest I have a duty of care for those to whom I minister and that for some this atmosphere of enquiry and exploration is uncomfortable. I hope I am able to strike a good balance between judicious investigation into what it means to be a follower of Jesus and reassurance that we can trust God to look after us in our quest.

3

We All Fall Down

There is a serious omission in the training of priests concerning the management of property. In theory the care of the church building is down to the churchwardens but these days there is such pressure on volunteer time that even if you are able to find people willing to take on such an important role, their availability will often be severely limited and expecting them to take on the huge responsibility of an ancient building, or two or more, is a big ask. Maybe it's just me, but I feel a responsibility to look after the assets of the church and cannot help getting involved when I see a repair is necessary or the building can be improved in some way. I do know some vicars who are blissfully ignorant of the state of the building they worship in every week and are equally unaware of the finances of the congregation, but I think these are few and far between.

My introduction to church building management began with our rather dilapidated church hall. Unusually, this was not situated on the same plot as the church but was three streets away, nestled in a row of terrace houses right in the heart of the parish. The church was originally acquired for the Church of England by a visionary priest who persuaded the diocese to buy it from a woman who had bought it for her son but then been thwarted in her ambition for him to become the priest by a series of protests in the parish (a hint of things to come). Shortly after the purchase in 1875 there was a rapid building programme in the area to accommodate all the workers needed to staff the train sheds built alongside Brighton station to build and maintain trains on the popular London to Brighton line. The Revd. George Hewitt seized an opportunity for the church to take up some land in a new street being built nearby and managed to build a church hall which was seamlessly incorporated into the row of houses as though it was just a triple length house. This hall was to become a Sunday school, complete with separate entrances for boys and girls, toilets and some small classrooms alongside the main hall.

This hall had variously been used as a Sunday School, mission hall, Boy's Brigade and Brownies venue, nursery and playschool and was much loved by the community of families who lived in the streets around. When I arrived, it was mostly used for children's birthday parties, occasional community meetings and local community groups. The congregation only used it on Sunday mornings when any children who came along to church would leave the service at some point to walk ten minutes to the hall, rain or shine, spend ten minutes having a class and then walk another ten minutes back to church. As church usage was so low it was not looked after particularly well and the meagre hire fees from other events only just covered the cost of utilities and insurance so there was no money for any repairs or maintenance.

A few weeks after being licensed to my new post I thought I would survey my empire and visit the hall to see what it was like. I entered a lovely, light building with a timber framed roof and stripped wooden floor, which had the faintly musty smell so often found in church halls. A tour around confirmed that the toilets were disgusting and appeared to be constantly leaking as well as harbouring various types of green mould;, the kitchen was falling apart and was not particularly clean; and there appeared to be a variety of damp patches scattered around the building. I noticed that there was quite a lot of loose plaster high up on some of the walls and a few small piles of dust on the hall floor and some of this plaster looked very precarious. I eventually found a broom in a part of the girl's toilets, detached the brush and proceeded to go around the space poking any bits of loose plaster I could see, very quickly covering myself in dust and chunks of wall. Thank goodness it was me being bombarded by bits of masonry and not some four-year-old child having a party or an elderly pensioner attending a history night. This was a health and safety nightmare!

The rest of my afternoon was spent whacking every bit of wall I could reach and poking and prodding everywhere that looked a bit unsafe until I had piles of rubble all over the floor which I shovelled up and bagged up ready for the tip. Eventually I was content that everything was as safe as I could make it and I had a good clean up ready for the next set of users. It was clear to me that some more drastic action than a vicar with a big stick was needed for a long-term solution. So, I contacted an architect friend who works on churches and church halls to ask him to come and look at the building and give me an opinion on what we needed to do. He looked around the building for about ten minutes, pursing his lips and tutting occasionally without saying anything, and eventually turned to me and said 'You need to get rid of this liability as soon as you can!' This wasn't quite the answer I was expecting and it put me in a bit of a quandary because one of the first contacts I had with a parishioner was to be invited out for coffee and a chat by someone whose sole purpose for the meeting was to get me to promise not to sell the church hall! It was already clear to me that this much-loved hall was important to the community but not to the congregation, who had enough on their plate looking after a much bigger and older church building and were not too bothered about premises that they hardly ever used or even visited.

The next question was, how do you go about selling a church hall and was the hall even ours to sell? I had sold houses before, or more correctly, my wife had as she is the one with the administrative and financial skills for a task such as this. Was it just the same for a church building? I was able to confirm with the diocese that they had no material interest in the hall and that it belonged entirely to the church, so I began the process of asking the PCC what they thought. We had a fairly long discussion about this at one of our meetings and the general feeling was that it would be a good idea to sell the hall, especially as some of the council members were pretty infrequent visitors to the hall and all of them were concerned to learn of the poor state of the building. To make sure that everything was above board, I put a formal proposal to the meeting and asked for a vote which was passed unanimously.

A note about PCCs: every church has one, but these are not the same as a Parochial Council which is a civic committee for the benefit of the community often found in rural villages and in some towns. These days a PCC is usually registered as a charity (any church with income over £100,000 per year must register with the Charity Commission and churches with lower income may register) and so PCC members are trustees of that charity and therefore have to comply with charity law. This means that PCCs have to get the best possible return on any asset which they wish to dispose of. In the old days it used to be possible for organizations to give away assets to an appropriate organization for a nominal sum of £1 but this is not possible any more as such a transaction may be deemed inappropriate by the Charity Commission, who can levy a fine on charities who do not make the best use of their assets because this can be seen as financial mismanagement. As it turned out, our church hall was listed in our accounts as an asset worth £450,000 although this had never been tested on the market and so was a nominal sum.

In order to prove to the Charity Commission that we were doing our best to maximize the value of this dilapidated asset we had to put it on the open market, so through a member of the congregation we engaged the services of an estate agent. They in turn said that we needed a lawyer to sort out the legal status of the hall and to manage contracts of sale etc. I got in touch with the firm of lawyers that act as registrars for the diocese as I thought they would be best placed to provide advice relevant to our sale. They were happy to act for us and I received a whole slew of questions about land registry, title deeds and charitable purposes. This was turning into a full-time job, and I was rapidly having to learn about lots of subjects I had never encountered before. I did manage to work out that original documents about the hall were lodged with the East Sussex archive and after a day of searching came away with enough paperwork to satisfy the solicitors.

The recommendation of the estate agent was that we put the hall up for sale using a closed bid system with a defined deadline. This meant that any interested buyer had to submit a bid direct to the estate agent who would collect sealed bids up to the date defined and then have a discussion with us about which bid we would like to accept. The first question I had from the estate agent was did we want a 'For Sale' board to go up outside the hall. I naively thought this was a good idea in the spirit of transparency and openness that I understood the Charity Commission wanted, so I agreed to this. The board duly went up and within days all hell broke loose!

Never underestimate the passion a community may have when it comes to issues of property, planning, developers or the perceived interests of their neighbourhood. Within weeks of the sale boards going up I began to hear rumours of discontent in the community. Then someone who I knew from our local community association contacted me to ask if I would meet a few concerned neighbours to begin a dialogue about the sale. I agreed and consequently the churchwardens and myself met half a dozen locals in the church so that they could see the potential for it to be used as a community space just as much as the hall was. To my surprise their biggest concern was that we would sell the hall to a developer who would knock it down and erect a block of flats in the middle of the street, and by their estimate this could net the church over a £1million! Much as I would have loved that much money to secure the future of the church and allow us to employ staff to grow and develop our work, I had already been told by the estate agent that it was extremely unlikely that the council would approve planning permission for a property which was a community asset, especially as we had put an overage clause into the sale terms which meant that 50 per cent of any profit made from a development of this nature would have to be paid to the church. The neighbours were somewhat appeased when they realized we were doing all that we could to ensure that the hall would remain available to them in some form and they seemed to go away reassured.

My hopes that this would be the end of any debate were short-lived as very quickly I got news that a petition was being circulated. Alongside this, residents banded together to form a committee of interested persons who started meeting regularly to make plans and keep each other up to date with progress.

I continued to engage with a few of the residents by email and after a bit of to-ing and fro-ing we agreed to hold a public meeting in the hall so that I could explain the church's reasoning behind selling the hall and give people a chance to ask questions.

The evening of the meeting arrived and I found myself standing in front of over a hundred local people who were mostly pretty angry with me as the principal protagonist in this project to sell 'their' hall. It didn't matter to them that the hall wasn't theirs but belonged to the church and that we had to fulfil our obligations to the Charity Commission in running an open sale process. As far as the community was concerned, I was trying to make a ton of cash by denying them somewhere to hold their children's birthday parties and to spoil their quaint local street with a monstrous block of flats. My churchwardens and a few other church members sat in the meeting but wisely decided that their best contribution was to leave the talking to me, especially once they saw that the meeting was getting quite heated. So I defended our decision from the front with as much clarity and grace as I could.

There then followed weeks of tense discussion and communication as emails flew around the parish, a campaign to save the hall was set up and the estate agent got on with their job of showing interested parties around the building and accepting sealed bids. I found myself fielding all sorts of angry responses that came to me in a variety of ways including a mother who sat in my study berating me for destroying the community while her children sat on the floor playing with a selection of toys I'd provided. My wife got used to telling me that there was someone else at the door who had come to shout at me about the church hall. I couldn't go into any of the pubs in the parish without someone having a go at me for being the worst vicar in living memory and the reason that the church was in decline.

The day of the deadline for bids arrived and I hoped that this might bring some sort of resolution to this awful time of tension and discord, but sadly not. We had eight bids, a number of which came close to the £400,000 asset price we had in our accounts, but also one from the community for the princely sum of £1. This came with a letter explaining this was a placeholder while the group worked to raise funds in order to place a better offer on the table. Unfortunately, we had to consider what we felt was the best offer on the closing date for the bids and at a subsequent PCC meeting it was decided to accept an offer from a circus school which put a good amount of cash on the table and also promised to continue the use of the hall as a community venue. This seemed like a great offer to us and fulfilled our need to satisfy the Charity Commission and would keep the hall available to the locals for all the same activities that were being hosted there.

I breathed a sigh of relief because it looked as though we had a solution that everyone could be happy with and we could all move on, but my peace was short-lived as it became clear that this was not the result that the community wanted and they weren't going to give up campaigning for a different outcome. In many respects things began to get even more tense as I sought to negotiate with the successful bidder but the community campaign got stronger. It had now reached the press and the local newspaper was running stories about the plucky community group that was fighting the nasty old church to ensure the safety of their beloved community hall. I felt more beleaguered than before and trying to conduct the normal business of the church alongside complicated legal and commercial negotiations took up every minute of my day.

As the chair of the PCC and vicar of the church I felt a personal responsibility to be the person who took all the criticism during this difficult period. Expecting volunteer churchwardens and PCC members, who only step into these roles because of their commitment to Jesus, to put themselves in the firing line for something so contentious and stressful feels unfair to me. As the only person being paid to be at the church, I have always felt that it should be me who takes the frontline responsibility and whatever fallout there might be. I don't know if this is what is at the heart of servant leadership but Jesus certainly gives us a model of living that includes an element of taking flak on behalf of others. If substitutionary atonement is at the heart of your understanding of salvation, then this should lead to this kind of sacrificial leadership, shouldn't it?

Eventually the stress of this difficult community argument became too much for the successful bidder and the circus school pulled out of the negotiations, taking us back to square one as none of the other bidders were appropriate or prepared to go through the process again. So that left us with the community bid of £1 which we couldn't accept without getting a slap on the wrist and possibly a fine from the Charity Commission. The PCC met again and decided to pause the process for six months to give the local residents time to raise enough money to make a credible bid. They had got themselves well organized by this time and set up an official organization and began fund raising by selling shares. Many people rallied behind this and money gradually began to come in as people bought shares, helped by some support from our local MP. Members of the church also became shareholders as a sign of our commitment to helping this process along and relations between the church and the parish slowly began to improve.

As the six-month extension got close, I consulted our friendly property surveyor about an appropriate valuation of the hall, which had descended into a greater state of disrepair over the intervening time as any attempt at maintenance had stopped while the future of the hall was so uncertain. Given this and the market proof that it was not possible to sustain a valuation as high as before, we were able to get a professional valuation of £200,000 which made the target for the community fundraising much more achievable. I also wanted to ensure that some church activities still had a guaranteed right to use the hall and so we proposed a side agreement to the contract of sale that reserved the use of the hall for Brownies, Boy's Brigade and Sunday morning Sunday school. We also inserted a clause into the contract restricting the eventual owners from selling on the property and giving the church right of first refusal if this became necessary. In return for these conditions we would offer a £50,000 discount to the sale price, neatly bringing the cost of the hall to £150,000 which happened to be the amount the community had raised.

At last we were able to put together the formal paperwork, get signatures and arrange bank transfers and the hall was sold. Two years of wrangling, at least a dozen PCC meetings, three public meetings, hundreds of emails and lots of discussion with individuals, groups and committees resulted in the transfer of the hall into community ownership. During that time I lost a church treasurer who felt I was steamrolling the PCC into disposing of a church asset at an unreasonable price and being too kind to the community, I had avoided going into any local pubs for a year, I'd been shouted at by a variety of local residents and supported by wonderful churchwardens.

The week after completing the sale it was discovered that one of the back rooms was riddled with dry rot and the whole back of the building had to be closed off. If it had still been in our possession, we would have had to close the whole building and it would have remained closed for ages as we had no money to treat such a serious problem. The community interest group which now owned the hall did have some cash reserves thanks to our generous discount and so were able to rectify the dry rot and over the ensuing years have been able to make major improvements to the building, putting on a new roof, installing new toilets and putting in better heating.

The church was able to earmark the cash from the hall sale as seed money for a major church re-ordering project that made the church building into a much more useful and accessible community asset complete with disabled access ramps and a fully-accessible toilet. Today both buildings complement each other in contributing to the communal life of the parish of Prestonville. We work together to play to the particular strengths of each building, the church providing meals to those in need and hosting various recovery projects and family activities, choirs and public meetings, while the former hall provides a regular home for Pilates, table tennis, art classes and job clubs as well as being a great venue for social events and parties.

The journey to this place of harmony and collaboration was hard fought and caused many sleepless nights but the end result has come to be seen as a model of how to ensure that a community can benefit from changes such as this and the process has become a case study for other groups around the country who are also trying to do good things for their neighbourhoods in the face of increasing commercialization and stripping of community assets for commercial gain.

The Church of England is in a unique position due to its foundation as a network of parishes that cover the whole country ensuring that it has a presence in every city, town and village. Churches and church halls are important havens of communal use and demonstrate the presence of God, whether this is recognized by residents or not. The path to community regeneration may not always be easy, but it is a journey worth taking even if it can feel like the path that Jesus took to the cross as we seek to do what is right for our church congregations as well as the parishes we serve. But it is a path of servant leadership (and sometimes vilification and pain) which can reflect the kind of humble service that Jesus showed to his disciples.

4

We All Build Up

One of the things I found hard to believe ahead of becoming a parish priest was that anyone would trust me with a church building. The thought of being given a set of keys to such an important asset and having free rein with it was quite daunting. I'm not sure I would have trusted me with something like this. Even as an adult I often felt that I wasn't mature enough to own a bicycle, let alone an ancient building six times the size of an average house. Little did the church know that my past included the decision to knock a wall down in the first house we owned without any knowledge of building management, structural surveys or even tools – all I possessed was a big hammer! It wasn't until the wall was down and I stood knee deep in rubble that I thought to ask my wife if we even had a shovel. This was followed by umpteen trips to the dump with bricks and plaster in the boot of our little Mini Metro which ended up doing serious damage to the suspension.

Becoming a parish priest includes taking full responsibility for the church building, in theory shared with the churchwardens, but when you live in a vicarage right next to the church the job description necessarily extends to being church caretaker, keyholder, odd job maintenance person and security guard. None of these roles are covered when we train as a priest; the clue to that is in the name of the institutions which provide ministerial training. Wannabe priests are sent to theological college where they learn about doctrine, Church history, biblical studies, liturgy, pastoral work, philosophy and ancient languages such as Greek and Hebrew. In my experience these are mostly unused subjects in parish ministry and at least some of the time at college would have been much better spent learning about building management, simple plumbing skills, basic carpentry and electrics and how to write a planning application for both a local authority and the arcane church planning process known as a faculty.

Having successfully sold the church hall, the church now had some cash in the bank and we were able to start work towards fulfilling the promise I had made to the parish that we would spend this on re-ordering the church to make it a more community-friendly space. As I began to explore this I discovered that almost every other vicar in the last 20 years had aspirations and dreams about the building, and scattered around in various files and folders in church cupboards there were at least three different schemes to significantly alter the building.

One scheme proposed that the vicarage should be knocked down and the west wall of the church opened up and extended to create a four-storey block which would include living quarters for the vicar, a couple of additional flats and some offices. Another scheme looked at cutting the church in half by inserting a floor along the whole length of the building so that the worship space would be on an upper floor using the whole property and the ground floor would become a small hall with offices and store rooms. None of these schemes had gone beyond the ideas phase, although one had got to a slightly more advanced stage and money had been raised to build a glass wall at the west end of the church so as to create a Sunday school room. Because this money had been donated for this particular purpose it could only be spent on a glass wall and so the cash sat in a restricted fund in our bank account, untouchable until we proceeded with some sort of glass wall, which meant that any future plan to change the building would have to include a transparent partition if we wanted to use that cash.

We were recommended to write a statement of needs as an outline brief for our architects to draw up some plans and after some discussion this is what the PCC came up with:

- Flexible main area for variety of uses (services, toddler groups, sports, dance, drama, concert space, exhibition space).

- Four breakout rooms of varying types.
- Kitchen and café facilities.
- Accessible WCs.
- Counselling/prayer room.
- Office.
- Storage space.
- Heating.
- Flexible seating.
- Security.
- Sound and visual facilities.
- Potentially open public lobby.

I look back on this list half a dozen years later and reflect that it is fairly conservative and practical but also that we have achieved most of this, the exceptions being breakout rooms and an office. This is a considerable success, no thanks to our architects who somehow managed to take this list and come up with a plan to knock down one of the church outbuildings and create a brand new entrance into the church from a completely different direction, complete with a two-storey block for a café and office and a gigantic glass atrium connecting this to the church! Beware of architects who have grand visions for your precious building and their bank account, which will look good in their portfolio rather than being a set of plans that can actually be implemented and won't cost an arm and a leg.

The plans did include all the things in our list and so we thought we'd apply for planning permission for the whole scheme, knowing that we would only be able to achieve some of it in the first phase of work. Major building work like this is subject to the same planning rules as any other building project and so this needed to be submitted to the local council for planning approval. In addition, the Church of England has its own planning process which involves applying to the diocesan chancellor, via the Diocesan Advisory Council, for what's called a faculty. Both these procedures are quasi-legal and have to be done correctly to ensure that the public know what's going on and have a chance to object or question any proposals.

My previous experience of church faculties had not been a happy one. The church I serve has a tower and spire and the tower has a set of oak louvres which are open to the elements to allow the sound of the church bell to be heard across the parish whenever it is rung. Unfortunately, being open so that sound can go out also meant that it was open so that birds could come in, which wasn't ideal for a part of the church housing a bell and an ancient clock. An attempt had been made to stop this ingress of nature a few years before by nailing some wire mesh to the inside of the louvres, but this simply created a perfect nesting place for pigeons. It also often trapped them and their young and the whole lot became clogged with old nests, feathers and dead birds. The floor directly below this was ankle deep in guano and the wood of the louvres was rotten and warped and needed to be replaced. There was clearly a lot to be done on this part of the building and it felt like something we needed to get on with before the worship space started to be invaded by baby pigeons and the smell of rotting bird mess.

So, one weekend, I and a churchwarden donned masks, overalls and boots and cleared as much filth from the tower as we could and I phoned around to find a company that did repairs and got one to come and do a survey and give us a quote. Their recommendation was to completely remove all the old oak, replace this with new louvres and then wrap the tower in bird-proof mesh and they proposed to do all this for £10,000 using a hydraulic lifting platform. I consulted the PCC and they agreed to this and so we gave them the go-ahead and a month later all the work was complete and we had a lovely new set of louvres and a bird-free tower and spire.

Six months later I was invited to join a training day for new vicars, something which I had been asking about since being licensed and was happy to join in with, despite it being two years after taking up the job. The first session was all about canon law and faculties and much to my dismay included the information that all work of over £3,000 had to have a faculty even if it was just a like for like repair! I felt a bit sick for the rest of the day as I wondered what to do about this. I did eventually confess to the Archdeacon a few weeks later that one of my first major projects as a parish priest may have transgressed Church law due to my ignorance. He reassured me that he could solve this misdemeanour by dividing the project into separate pieces of work so that they could each be approved by him because clearly this was an improvement to the building and had been done well and in good faith.

So, I approached the necessity to do both council and church planning paperwork with some trepidation. With the help of the architects, I prepared papers and plans, budget estimates and legal notices and we proceeded to submit packs of papers to the relevant authorities. As our plans included this ambitious scheme to build a new entrance and atrium, I thought it would be polite to let the neighbours know about this, particularly as there was one house directly adjoining the development. The house was divided into flats and so I wrote a polite letter to all the occupants inviting them to the vicarage one evening for a glass of wine and to see our plans.

The evening started well as we got to know each other over drinks and found out a little about our various backgrounds and then I got the papers out to show them our ideas. I thought the plans were fairly uncontroversial but as I explained them there was a distinct darkening of the mood in the room. As soon as I had finished one of the residents exploded, saying this was a disgrace and that this scheme would only go ahead over his dead body! It seemed the other residents all agreed and the evening ended pretty abruptly with them all leaving with threats to set up a protest group and to resist these plans with all the energy they could muster – but not without finishing their wine first! It was a total shock to me, not to mention an abuse of our hospitality and our free wine and nibbles!

A little bit daunted by this response, I went ahead and submitted the planning proposal. Notice of this then gets sent to near neighbours and is posted on local lampposts etc. and once these had gone out objections started to roll in to the council planning website. There seemed to be quite a few of these but on closer inspection I could see they all came from the same set of residents that we'd invited to pre-inspect the plans. Shortly after that posters began appearing in the local streets exhorting residents to stand up to this terrible development and we discovered from a few neighbours that there was a door-to-door campaign to get people to sign some sort of petition against me. Fortunately, my relationship with most of the parishioners was good enough for them all to decline to join the anti-vicar movement.

As there were objections lodged to the council the application had then to be sent to the planning committee for discussion rather than just being nodded through by an officer. At committee the objectors are allowed to present their case for three minutes and I would be allowed to speak to their objections for a similar amount of time. The day came for the committee to meet and I went along to make sure my voice was heard only to discover that the objectors had declined the offer to speak, which also meant that I was denied the opportunity to speak. But I wasn't going to let this important meeting just go by without a presence from the church to witness the debate and pray for the decision makers. I was heartened to find I was sat at the back of the public seating area with one of the regular attendees at our monthly Sunday afternoon food drop-in, who told me he went to every council planning committee to ensure that proper procedure was followed.

I then sat through the most boring, detailed and frustrating six hours of my life, because our application was right at the end of the agenda. I listened to application after application being presented, discussed, debated and voted on including discussions about changing a shop into a pizza takeaway when there were already three in the same street through to major developers asking permission to build multi-storey blocks of flats. I gained enormous respect for local councillors who do this kind of thing every three weeks as part of their part-time job as councillors and take a lot of aggravation for it as well.

Finally, it came to our application and I nervously heard our plans described incorrectly! The officer presenting the case didn't seem to understand our plans and was giving the councillors terrible advice about our project. I was supposed to sit silently in the public area but couldn't contain myself and stood up to offer clarification and set the record straight. It helped that I was wearing my clerical collar and it had been noted that I'd sat there for six hours waiting for this moment and that I knew a couple of the councillors through other community projects we had done together. Although strictly forbidden they did allow me to speak briefly so that I could correct the errors in presentation and eventually the item went to a vote and to my relief was passed.

Alongside this we also initiated the church planning process, which involved sending sets of plans and a description of the work to the Chancellor of the Diocese and posting a notice about the work in a public place for 28 days. There was one thorny issue which was of particular concern and this was what to do with the font. Fonts are typically close to the main door of a church because baptism symbolizes entry into the family of faith. Our font was right in the middle, close against the west wall of the church. The recommendation of the architect and the Diocesan Advisory Council was to remove it completely and either commission a new font for a different part of the church or use a portable one which we already possessed.

In preparing the papers for this application I discovered that fonts can't simply be thrown away or given to an architectural salvage company to sell or even moved into a garden to become a bird bath or ornamental pond. These would all be examples of 'unseemly use' or transfer into 'unsuitable hands', which wasn't allowed. There is a commonly held belief that the recommended method of disposal is to bury it on church land, although I discovered that this is only an option of last resort. I included a question to the Chancellor in our application asking for his suggestion about an appropriate method of disposal. This turned out to be redundant as he refused permission to remove the font and so we had to redo our plans to find another solution.

In the meantime I set about finding a contractor to do the work. It's good practice to get at least three quotes and I asked the architect's advice for suitable companies and was given a list of builders who were all based at least 40 miles away from us – some were on the other side of London! In the end I got a couple of recommendations of local companies from friends and we sent out a tender to these and one or two from the architect's list. Consequently, we ended up choosing a middle of the range quote from a local company and set up a contract to begin work.

The first phase was a complete redesign of the main entrance and the west end of the church, so we had to work out how to continue to use the church while the work was going on. The solution was to turn the whole church round and use a fire exit at the east end of the church as the main entrance and build a temporary internal wall across the west end so that the builders could get on with their work behind this wall with no interruption to worshipping in the church on Sundays and all the midweek activities.

We were all set to begin work when the paperwork came back from the Chancellor approving everything except the removal of the font! We had no historical information about the font, which appeared to be one big lump of sandstone and could have come from another church and be older or have some sort of historical significance, so the chancellor thought it wiser to keep it. This answer had taken so long to arrive that we'd already signed with the contractor and agreed a start date so I had to rush out another 28-day public notice with a revision of the plans and didn't have time to go through another design phase with the architects so just decided to leave it where it was, which would become a separate room at the back of church eventually called the Font room.

All in all, the admin to get this project going from drawing up plans at the start to actually getting spades in the ground (literally) took almost 18 months, which was just as well because we also had to raise some extra money to do this, despite having set a budget and asked everyone to work within that.

Finally work began and we got used to using the church back to front, which was just as well because the three-month project begun in May turned into a 6-month project that ran into the winter and was beginning to look like it wouldn't be finished for Christmas, which would have been tricky as I'd booked the bishop to come and officially bless the new entrance and rooms in late November.

WE ALL BUILD UP

The building work seemed to get slower as time progressed, not helped by me interfering, or as the architect described it 'getting a bit picky'! It started with a new wall alongside the wheelchair ramp being built as part of the entrance. For some reason the architect's design had the retaining wall for the ramp narrowing towards the top of the slope with a weird return stub of a wall at right angles at the top. I tried to stop the bricklayer as he was building this but he showed me the plans and assured me that was what the architect wanted. On the next visit from said architect I asked why there was this odd skewed design and got the reply 'it's quirky, like Brighton'! This didn't seem a good enough reason to have a ramp that got more difficult to navigate as you went up it so I insisted that the wall be knocked down and built again.

Then we came to internal fittings and I'm not a great one for details but there were some things that even I noticed. We'd been able to create a new meeting room as part of the re-ordering but when it was almost complete and the one remaining builder was decorating it, I noticed that only one wall had a skirting board, all the other walls just ended in a rough plastered edge at the tiled floor. Another question was sent to the architect who seemed to think it was the most outrageous idea that all four walls of a room should have a skirting board! Another detail was the beautiful new fully-accessible toilet which was big enough for full-sized electric wheelchairs as well as double buggies. It was fitted with everything you'd expect for a disabled facility such as rails beside the toilet and an alarm if someone needed assistance. The only trouble was that the door lock was a simple round twist knob, difficult to use for an able-bodied person and absolutely impossible for anyone with a disability or arthritis.

The work got slower and slower towards the end until we just had one elderly carpenter on site who kept telling me he had come back from retirement but was doing this to help out. Although he was a carpenter it was apparent that he was responsible for everything, building walls, plastering, fixing door frames, final bits of plumbing and all the decorating. Alongside this very slow progress I was getting increasingly frantic demands from the contractor to pay the final invoices as soon as they were issued. The one worker would disappear off for days at a time and rarely spent a whole day at the church, and then I heard through one of our PCC members who was also an architect that the contractor had stopped work on a big project they had in progress. It wasn't long before we heard that the company had gone into administration, which was a terribly sad situation for those who were employed by them and for other projects which were only halfway through, so I felt fortunate that they'd pretty much completed their work with us and we were able to set a date for a grand re-opening.

We managed to book our suffragan bishop to come and bless the renewed building one Sunday morning and decided to have a big celebration including a hog roast lunch. The day before when I was helping the supplier unload the whole pig he'd sourced for us I became aware of the disapproval of people walking past as we hauled this big hunk of pork across the pavement into the church. It seemed the vegetarian-leaning folk of our part of Brighton weren't great fans of overt displays of meat eating but I was slightly vindicated the next day when I saw my Jewish friends from the progressive synagogue tucking in with great relish after the service! It was great to celebrate the end of this construction project and the blessing to the church over the years since then in having these new facilities has been well worth the effort.

5

The Joy of Sex in Church

The Church is obsessed with sex – I've never been in any organization that focused so much on sex. For an institution that includes some who feel called to a life of celibacy there is an unhealthy fascination with wanting to know who is doing it, how they are doing it, what's the relationship between those who do it and how can we codify it. We never seem to stop talking about it and we've even had formal groups convened to discuss it. In my experience this began with a series of facilitated discussions known as the Shared Conversations process, although of course it has been a topic of conversation for Christians ever since the Church began. The Shared Conversations project started with bishops chatting among themselves in 2014, followed by 'conversation' groups held in dioceses in 2015 and then with General Synod members later in 2015.

Never being one to feel left behind by a trend, I thought it would be a good idea to have some discussions of our own while this was going on across England, so in 2014 I contacted a guy called Steve Chalke to ask if he would come and speak at St Luke's. Steve is a Baptist minister who is fairly outspoken and has a talent for getting into the news by speaking out. He'd been pretty vocal about same sex-marriage and that the Church should welcome homosexual couples and give them the same right to get married as we do heterosexual couples. He is also an evangelical and so I thought it would be good to get him to come to St Luke's to explain his position and help us think about this controversial topic. I vaguely knew him from the Greenbelt arts, faith and justice festival and so I contacted him with this idea and Steve readily agreed and a date was set.

I let the PCC know about this plan and very shortly afterwards started to receive letters of complaint. What surprised me most was the argument these letters took, which was characterized by the assertion that this was a subject that we shouldn't talk about. I'd never come across the idea that there were things that a Christian just shouldn't say, except perhaps certain types of swearing. These letters gave the idea that talking about same-sex relationships was somehow dangerous or inappropriate for a Christian. They even suggested that this was an unsuitable topic to be talking about in church and that if I insisted on pursuing this then I should hire an alternative venue rather than pollute the church building with this sort of talk. I couldn't understand the fear that was inherent in some of these letters, that somehow by talking about this important subject we'd be doing something evil, allowing the devil to set foot in our church and setting a bad example to those around us. This was particularly weird given we are based in Brighton, the unofficial LGBTQI+ capital of the UK.

These letters did contain one good suggestion though, and that was to have more than one speaker so that a range of views could be expressed rather than just hearing one side of the sexuality debate. So, I began to hunt around to find a suitable second speaker to provide a counter-balance to the debate. I fairly quickly discovered a lecturer in theology called Sean Doherty who was equally prominent in the debate about sexuality and the Church because he is attracted to men but is married to a woman and has a family. I contacted him and explained what I was aiming to do and discovered that Sean was available on the date we had set and so I tentatively booked him in. This was followed with a telephone call for us to flesh out some of the detail and to check in with each other on the kind of themes that might be touched on during the evening.

I discovered that Sean had an interesting point to make about the particularity of relationships versus the generality of sexuality. He told me that his sexual orientation was towards men but that human beings form relationships with particular individuals and he had the divine fortune to have fallen in love with a particular woman and so was quite comfortable being in a married relationship with his wife while still recognizing that his general orientation was geared towards those of the same sex as him. I thought this was an interesting position and would make for a great discussion on the night and so I reshaped the format of the evening to include both Sean and Steve.

I billed this as an opportunity to listen to two experts in the field air the issues around this subject in an open and honest way. I agreed with them that they would each have 15 minutes to talk about their understanding of same-sex relationships, Church and marriage, which would then lead into an open conversation between the two of them in front of an audience who would be invited to ask questions at the end.

On the day they both arrived early in Brighton because I'd suggested we have supper together before the event so that they would have a chance to chat and get to know each other a little. We had a pleasant meal talking about shared acquaintances and connections and lightly touching on some of the themes of the evening before going into the church. I fiddled about getting them fixed up with microphones and checking the PA as the church gradually filled up until we had a capacity crowd.

Sean began with some of his personal story and his understanding that while Jesus loved and accepted everyone, he didn't always leave them where they were but often took people on a journey. He also wanted to make it clear that he felt that sex is a gift from God to be enjoyed within marriage between a man and a woman, which was the most appropriate place to be having children. Steve took a completely different tack and proposed that these debates about sexuality were not about sex at all but about our understanding and interpretation of the Bible. He declared that evangelicals don't really read the Bible critically but do love to quote it (usually out of context) while ignoring the contradictions that exist in this library of diverse literature. The discussion between the two of them was lively, humorous and thought-provoking and was followed by some interesting questions from the audience. I closed the evening with a prayer and an invitation to all present to continue the discussion.

I felt the evening had gone well, it had been respectful of a range of positions and had aired the most important views about this topic and no-one had got hot under the collar or stormed out, both actions which I had feared might be the outcome. From my perspective the issue had been debated in an open and honest way and we could move along as a church without worrying about it again. How wrong could I be!

Fairly soon after the evening I began to receive messages about this topic which showed the diversity of opinion within our congregation. Some wanted us to make what they called a clear, unequivocal statement on same-sex relationships without saying anything about what that statement should be, the implication being it should be in favour of 'traditional' marriage. Others declared that they couldn't be part of a church that condoned homosexual practice, sometimes suggesting that people should be helped to give up these 'sinful' ways of living and that we shouldn't pander to the views of society at large. Others expressed gratitude for an open and honest debate and appreciated a thoughtful approach to interpreting Scripture and genuine pastoral concern for those who might be forced into celibacy or promiscuity because of the church position on their God-given sexuality.

I collected up some of these comments and we continued discussions about this with the PCC. I even drew up a list with an indication of who thought what, discovering that around 50% of the congregation were in favour of same-sex marriage, 25% were against it, 15% were unsure, and 10% were unknown to me. I started to collect literature about this subject and provided it to anyone who asked for more information. As time went on the heat of discussion began to dissipate and it became less and less part of church conversations, largely because there was no real-life necessity for us to do anything about it. No same-sex couples were asking to get married in our church and no-one in the congregation was openly LGBTQI+ or living in a same-sex relationship. I realized that I had stirred up a hornet's nest of argument when the reality of our situation didn't need us to take any specific action, despite all our chatter.

Slowly the issue died down and I think this is the case with many church congregations. They might be aware that there is a discussion going on among clergy and bishops, a few very vocal lay people and at General Synod, but the reality on the ground at that time was that there was no lived experience of this at parish level and most people in church didn't know anyone who was openly in a same-sex relationship and didn't want to engage with an issue that wasn't relevant to them or their usual Sunday practice. One of the issues for the Church when discussing a topic such as this is the lack of personal experience and it's striking to me that so many people who have changed their minds about sexuality and the Church often do so as a result of a family member coming out as LGBTQI+. Once you meet someone who is personally impacted by impersonal, generic Church statements about sexuality, the Bible and lifestyle it's much harder to stick to bland generalizations dictating what other people should do. This is how the issue came home to roost for us.

St Luke's has a strong focus on being as family friendly as possible and when it's possible we try to put that focus into practice by employing someone to work with children and young people. We are all aware that congregations in the Church of England are becoming older and older and a high percentage have no children in attendance at all. We believe that churches need to put their money where their mouth is when it comes to creating a younger church and thanks to a generous legacy from one of our congregation, we were able to recruit a children's worker.

A job description was drawn up, ads placed on various websites and we received a number of applications and conducted interviews. Among the candidates was a young woman who was clearly talented and enthusiastic and seemed a really good fit but unfortunately she wasn't available to fit our timeframe as she was a student at a theological college known to be evangelical and conservative. So we employed the next best candidate but it was clear fairly quickly that this was not a good fit and so we mutually agreed to part company after six months. This then meant that the aforementioned woman was now available because her course was coming to an end, which seemed ideal. We conducted another interview and arranged for her to visit one Sunday to get a feel for us and to meet the PCC. The visit went really well and the PCC were really enthusiastic, with at least one member telling me how great it was to meet such a spirit-filled, evangelical young person with such a passion for working with young people. We took a formal vote on whether to continue discussions and all were in favour so we proceeded to let her know and to move on to the next phase of drawing up a contract of employment.

We then hit a problem. She wrote back to me to say how much she'd enjoyed her visit and felt God calling her to work with us but she felt she ought to let us know that she was in a relationship with another woman and if she was appointed, they would be coming to Brighton together. This was not a surprise to me, although we had never had a conversation about this. While appreciating her honesty I could also see that this disclosure would be problematic because some of the most enthusiastic supporters of employing her were also well known to me as being among those who opposed the sexuality debates we'd been having. Having received this news I knew that I had to inform the churchwardens and the PCC before we signed any contracts.

Consequently, as we had a short PCC meeting planned immediately after her visit to confirm her in post, I phoned the churchwardens to let them know about this development so that they were forewarned. At the meeting I let everyone know of her disclosure and there followed a lively debate covering some of the ground we'd begun discussing at the shared conversations evening but also including celibacy, the importance of church leaders being a good example and the morality of religious workers co-habiting with partners, whatever their sexuality. Some people thought that we should produce a definitive statement about where we stood on the issue of sexuality but this was resisted by the majority as pushing an agenda onto a specific item of business that wasn't appropriate. We agreed to proceed to the next stage and would arrange for a second visit so that we could introduce her to our parent/toddler group and youth club to see how she fitted in. Alongside this PCC members would canvass the congregation and I would take some legal advice.

I let our suffragan bishop know what was going on and sought advice from our Archdeacon who confirmed that secular law applied in the case of youth workers and that it was not permissible to make a decision based on the sexuality of the candidate. Alongside this I received a couple of essays from one of the congregation arguing against her appointment on theological and social cohesion grounds and pointing out that we would be condoning immoral behaviour if we appointed her. I circulated these to all of the PCC along with some further reading about sexuality and the Bible.

A few weeks later the planned visit to our parent/toddler group and youth club took place with representatives from the PCC popping in to observe and chat with the candidate. Once again it was agreed that she was an excellent choice for the job and got on really well with the children and their families and those present fed back their positive views to the PCC. Following this visit we then held a special PCC meeting after church one Sunday where we had another full and frank discussion and eventually held a vote, with the overwhelming majority being in favour of employing her. The next day I wrote confirming her employment and sending a contract, final job description and information about starting dates etc. The PCC also asked me to produce an open letter to the whole congregation explaining what was going on and letting everyone know that I was available for one-to-one conversations about this with anyone who wanted them.

Overall, the PCC met three times to vote on this, with every vote being a majority in favour of moving ahead with employment. I had individual conversations with most members, some of whom told me they would resign if we went ahead with employment and others who told me they would resign if we didn't go ahead. The whole process was documented in minutes and the Archdeacon and bishop were kept informed because I felt it was really important that we followed a clear and transparent process so that everyone felt heard and understood but that there could be no complaint that we had not followed proper procedures. I also had to acknowledge that for some there was a great deal of hurt and disappointment at the eventual outcome which I could not address pastorally as those who were wounded by this saw me as the cause of their distress.

Unfortunately, a result like this sets up a situation where people are seen as winners or losers and it's impossible for the chief 'winner' to be able to offer comfort to those who see themselves as the losers of the argument. In that situation it's next to impossible to continue to offer any form of ministry to those in distress and since I was not going to leave my job, it meant that a significant proportion of the congregation decided to leave. However, that decision was never communicated to me, people simply stopped coming and so our Sunday numbers fell by about a third over the course of a month or so. In all I think that we lost almost half of our congregation over this issue, which pains me because my version of inclusive church includes those who disagree with me. I like to think that our differences over sexuality, ordination, doctrine and practice would all be trumped by our unity in Christ and I value a lively debate with people I don't necessarily see eye to eye with. Our church is a poorer place if it is full of people who all agree with each other and true inclusivity has room for those with whom we disagree. Sadly not all Christians agree with that.

I began to hear rumours that some who regarded themselves as leaders of the distressed were planning on starting a church of their own and they were discussing renting the former church hall on Sunday mornings to hold services. This was ironic as the hall now belonged to the community and this former Sunday school was an avowedly secular space with clear policies around inclusion and diversity which included not allowing any use of the hall by people who were homophobic. It also felt a bit vindictive as none of those discussing this lived in the parish or anywhere near the hall and setting up so close to our church building would have definitely been seen as a competitive move. Also, it would have violated Church of England rules if the new church was billed as being anything to do with Anglicanism. Fortunately, none of this came to pass and those who left St Luke's found homes in other churches across the city. I now see this as a form of gift as those people took their talent and their energy as a blessing to other churches and added to their congregations.

One of the things that the Church doesn't address very well is the huge number of de-churched folk that are around. Research generally tells us that around 30 per cent of the population are de-churched – people who used to go to church and were sometimes very heavily involved, but now don't. The reasons for leaving church are various and include moving house, having children and falling out with the minister. Disagreeing with the priest or having an argument with him/her is quite a common reason for leaving a church, I have done it myself, and it is a very painful thing to go through. Congregations are often very demanding of their priests and priests can sometimes be quite obnoxious to their congregations. We're all human after all and need to recognize that in our dealings with each other while also understanding that sometimes relationships do break down and we need to find ways to sensitively go our separate ways. Maybe the Church needs a form of divorce counselling alongside its discipleship courses and confirmation classes?

There was some additional fallout as it became clear that some of the dispossessed had decided to make some formal complaints about me. This can be a very serious thing as the only formal complaint process available for clergy is what's called a Clergy Discipline Measure. This is a semi–judicial process which can result in suspension or even dismissal from post for serious misdemeanours. Fortunately for me, I was simply informed that a letter had been sent to the Archbishop of Canterbury which had been passed down to my bishop and then my Archdeacon, who already knew what had been going on as I had kept them fully informed and followed correct procedures all the time.

I did get a call from our patrons who are an evangelical organization. They had also received a letter accusing me of railroading the church into employing this person. They carefully pointed out that they were only patrons and couldn't interfere with the work of the PCC and politely informed me that they were signed up to the Evangelical Alliance statement on sexuality and that I should have a look at it. I let the caller know that the PCC had voted on this appointment three times and always been in favour of going ahead with employment, at which point they let me know that they were unaware of this and that the complainant had given them the impression that I had overruled the PCC. With that the call ended and I have heard no more but there is a lingering worry in the back of my mind that when I eventually move on from this parish and the new incumbent is sought, the patrons will exercise more influence than they did at my appointment in order to reverse the journey towards inclusivity for all. This has been a problem for other churches in a similar situation.

Meanwhile at St Luke's we began a very fruitful working relationship with our new youth worker and her partner. Our youth club went from strength to strength, brilliant holiday clubs were organized during school holidays, assemblies took place in the local infant and junior schools and the young people in the church found themselves supported and befriended. Everyone loved having the couple around and the parish became aware that we didn't quite reflect the image of the national Church which was often portrayed as homophobic. This was further enhanced when the PCC decided we should join the Inclusive Church network, making us one of the early adopters of this outward sign of welcome among the churches in Brighton.

A year or so after they joined us, the couple let me know that they wanted to formalize their relationship and had decided to enter a civil partnership. They could have opted to get married because that became legal in the UK in 2013 and a church youth worker is not governed by Church rules that prohibit clergy from marrying a partner of the same sex. As is still the case at the time of writing, it is not possible for a same-sex couple to get married in a church or even have their civil marriage or civil partnership blessed in church but the couple wanted some sort of declaration of their commitment to each other to be acknowledged publicly before God. So, we began to plan a thanksgiving service.

At the time (2016) there was no liturgy or form of service to be used for such an occasion. I believe this was a deliberate decision by the Church of England because events for which there is no formal liturgy can therefore use forms of service created by the priest at their discretion. Once an official Church of England liturgy is produced, approved and formalized there is then no flexibility for priests because we declare at our licensing that we will only use authorized forms of service. Having no authorized liturgy avoided the difficulty the Church has had in discussions about appropriate forms of words in relation to the blessing of same sex relationships, as it wrestles with this issue and the desire of some of us for change.

This left us free to write a thanksgiving service of our own which followed a familiar format but definitely wasn't a wedding. I wrote my own preface to the service which made it very clear that the couple had entered a civil partnership the day before and that this was an opportunity to give thanks and celebrate their love for each other. I explicitly told everyone that if they ever found themselves chatting to a bishop or Archbishop they could tell them that this wasn't a wedding service or a blessing because sadly those are not allowed in the Church of England.

The final order of service was approved by the Archdeacon and the day before we decorated the church in preparation for the thanksgiving service and the celebration party that was to follow in the same building. The day itself was fabulous and the church was filled with family, friends and congregation members to celebrate with the happy couple. As is the case with every service, it ended with God's blessing for the whole congregation followed by cake and fizz and my first ever experience of a silent disco in church as we danced the night away.

The happy couple blessed us with their participation and their work for three years before we ran out of money and could no longer continue the post. During this time we had amazing children's work, wonderful holiday clubs and youth projects and formed great relationships with families and their children. We invented new opportunities to meet local young people as we gave out pancakes on Shrove Tuesday and hot chocolate on All Hallows Eve. They brought untold energy and Spirit-filled inspiration to our community and blessed us far more than we blessed them. Their presence enriched us and educated me and showed what the institution of the Church is missing by not fully embracing the gifts of service that so many same-sex couples wish to exercise in the Church. I look forward to the day when we can not only bless civil partnerships in church but perform weddings for all who wish to declare their love and commitment to each other before God.

6

Food, Waste and Compost

The central act of worship in many churches is communion, a symbolic meal that is intended as a re-enactment of the last supper that Jesus held with his closest friends, although in reality the tiny wafer of dried starch and minimal sip of fortified wine distributed in most churches wouldn't qualify in most homes as a supper and doesn't look much like the actual meal Jesus would have eaten. Nevertheless, there is some sort of connection between eating, community and faith and this has always been an important focus for me as the person who has the privilege of presiding over this symbolic meal. This combination of word, symbol and physical act embodies the essence of Christian faith, which involves and invades every part of our lives in our speech, in our vision and in our action. I believe churches should be a place of communal sharing of every part of our lives and eating together is an important part of that.

In late 2015 I heard about a group that had set up in Brighton called the Real Junk Food Project (RJFP) who were looking for more venues. Some people in our neighbourhood thought that this was an organization that produces unhealthy junk food but it's actually a charity that began in Leeds, rescuing food that would otherwise go to waste. They organize volunteers to collect food from supermarkets and restaurants that is just about to be thrown away for a variety of reasons. This food is then cooked into a nutritious hot meal and offered to anyone who would like to eat on a 'pay as you feel' basis. Often this means that individuals don't pay anything because they can't afford it and the project attracts lots of people in need or who are homeless, but it is also attended by families, students and anyone who is interested in more sustainable ways of living.

A small team had started a weekly lunch at a nearby Baptist church, which was very popular, and they were looking to expand the work and to find other venues for lunch and to use for storage. I thought this fitted well with St Luke's as we were already running a monthly Sunday afternoon drop-in for a hot meal and chat called The Carpenter's Arms and I could see the need for a service like this and felt that this was a way to extend our food offer beyond once a month.

So I contacted the organizers and invited them to come and visit and see what we could achieve together. The visit didn't take long and the small RJFP team snapped up the offer of using us as their second venue with an ambitious plan to open three days a week. They also loved the fact that we had a large balcony at the west end of the church which used to be the choir loft and could be used as a space for storage and some food prep. Within weeks they were moving tables into this space for chopping, peeling and prepping food and crates began to arrive full of potatoes, peppers, tomatoes and all manner of different types of food.

The lunches started early in 2016, serving from midday to 2pm every Monday, Tuesday and Wednesday and quickly grew so that 40–60 people were being fed every day. The driving force behind the project was a young guy who seemed to have endless amounts of energy and slaved away in the kitchen while a team of volunteers would descend on the church every day to help prepare food and serve it. Alongside this was another key person who would go out every evening in a small van and collect food from various supermarkets and take it all back to her flat to sort and organize before bringing it to the church first thing in the morning to be processed or stored.

Slowly the balcony began to fill up with crates that were stacked six–eight high, full of every type of food imaginable. Bulk packages of pasta and rice turned up along with boxes of tinned tomatoes, trays full of cauliflower and bags of onions. One of the things that surprised me was that there was always a lot of celeriac, I guess it's one of the ingredients that supermarkets feel they should stock but maybe customers don't know how to cook it so it quickly becomes surplus.

Something else began to happen slowly as the year moved on and spring turned to summer. I began to notice a few tiny flies attaching themselves to the linens covering the communion chalice on Sunday and found myself having to wave them away before distributing the wine. This gradually got worse and on some occasions I had to fish flies out of the wine as part of my preparation of the elements prior to distributing them. It felt as though we were at the beginning of some sort of biblical plague and I hoped that this wasn't a sign of God's displeasure. I mentioned this to the Junk Food team and suggested we investigate the stored food on the church balcony to find out what was going on. Starting with one of the stacks of crates, we lifted them off one by one to inspect the contents. Towards the bottom of one stack, we lifted the penultimate crate of the tower and a swarm of miniscule flies engulfed us. Their escape into the air revealed a mass of slowly liquefying potatoes in various states of decay, covered in mould and fur and not fit for consumption by any human being.

It turned out that the team had no process for rotating the crates and no-one wanted the bother of unstacking a whole tower of crates to ensure that the oldest potatoes got used first. I wondered if this was a parable of the church, a place where we continue to do what is easy and deal with the issues at the top of the pile rather than make the effort to dig down and find the people and situations that really need attention. It's much simpler to devote our time and energy to those who are right in front of us, those who are in our churches on a regular basis, those who present themselves to us, demanding our response. It's much harder to seek out those who are mostly invisible, those we never see, those whose difficulties are complex and intricate and will take longer for us to sort out. Yet these are the people and situations that Jesus chose to talk about, the shepherd who searched out the one sheep who'd gone astray, the widow who scoured the house for her lost coin.

After this investigation the volunteers put in a process for rotating the crates so that food didn't get left to rot. It took us some time to rid the church of flies and for most of that summer I had to keep a small bowl of communion wine on the communion table in addition to the chalice, this acted as a kind of fly trap and saved me having to fish struggling flies out of the symbolic blood of Jesus before distributing it to the congregation.

The Junk Food Project caused us more fly problems later that summer but this time outside the church. While their passion is to prevent food waste there is inevitably a degree of waste created in preparing meals with fresh food. Potato peelings need to go somewhere, onion skins have to be removed before an onion can be chopped, rotten tomatoes have to be disposed of and even the freshest produce can contain items that are only fit for the bin. I was keen that we tried to make use of this organic waste rather than just throw it away and so allocated a section of the church back garden to be used for composting. Unfortunately, I had massively underestimated the amount of waste that was generated from prepping fresh food for 50 people three days per week. Very quickly we had a compost heap almost entirely made up of vegetable peelings which was stacked up against a garden wall and stood almost 2m high. I had learned previously from a neighbour who was studying permaculture that good compost needed to be 50% cardboard but so much vegetable waste was being generated every week that we didn't have time to add cardboard even if we could have found enough for this burgeoning pile.

July in Brighton isn't necessarily tropical but it was warm enough that year for this huge pile of rotting veg to start incubating wildlife, principally in the form of maggots and flies. My wife and I had decided to celebrate our 30th wedding anniversary by taking a road trip across the US which would take most of the month, but a week into our trip I got a concerned email from our next-door neighbours, whose garden backed onto the wall where we were piling up compost. The smell and the flies had got so bad that they had to abandon a family barbecue in their own garden and retreat into the house to discover that it too was infested with flies! Quite rightly they asked that we do something about this immediately.

There followed a few panic emails to one of the churchwardens and the exchange of details of a waste management company who were paid to come out and spray the offending heap to try and calm down the plague of buzzing flies before removing the whole lot and disinfecting the garden. Such was the efficiency of their work and the pungency of the chemicals that the garden was not only cleared of all forms of rotten waste but also almost every form of natural life. It and the garden next door smelt of disinfectant for days afterwards, which meant the neighbours were still unable to use their garden for another week. Fortunately we had a good relationship with these neighbours as I had officiated at their wedding four years previously and baptized their daughter two years after that, but infesting their house and garden with flies did stretch our friendship quite a bit. Pastoral relationships formed in good times can be enormously important when things go wrong, as they inevitably will with any organization such as a church.

The Real Junk Food project settled into a good rhythm after these first few teething problems and the foundations they established with us gave them some stability and security which was important in consolidating this great work. I was astonished at the insight this gave me into the commercial operations of those who supply our food, although sometimes it was a bit inconvenient. My doorbell rang at 8am one Monday morning (my day off) with a truck driver asking where he should drop off some yoghurt drinks. Assuming it was a box or two I told him to bring them to the house only to be told that he wouldn't be able to get the palettes up the vicarage steps! It turned out there were two tonnes of drinks that had some sort of misprint on the cartons and so couldn't be sold to the public and were being donated to the project. After some head scratching, we settled on the palettes being dropped by the front door of the church and I quickly mobilized some volunteers to help unpack them and get them into the church. All the children at our local junior school got free yoghurt drinks that week!

Another revelation concerned business practice around home deliveries. One day I went into church to discover the volunteers poring over 25 crates from one of the major supermarkets with bags of home shopping in every one. It turned out these were part of a truckload of deliveries that had all missed their delivery times to homes because of a problem with the truck. It was not cost-effective for the supermarket to return all these deliveries to base and have someone sort it all through, re-bagging what was usable, disposing of items that had gone out of date or been unrefrigerated for too long and restocking ready for a return delivery. So this whole consignment, including bottles of wine, tins and all sorts of dried goods such as pasta, would have been simply thrown away. This insight into the waste that is accepted as part of commercial operation shocked me and made me grateful that the Real Junk Food Project was helping to rescue perfectly good food and use it for good. It also confirmed how right it was for us to be hosting such a project as part of our care for creation, doing our bit to help the environment and the wasteful practices that are hidden from us.

The service settled down and eventually became set on a regular timetable, serving a nutritious hot lunch every Tuesday and Wednesday to anyone who turned up. Often this meant feeding 80–100 people at each sitting and a small army of local volunteers grew up, faithfully attending from 9.30 in the morning ready to peel potatoes, chop carrots and assist our wonderful chef with any cooking prep that was needed. All the food preparation took place in a small back room which also provided storage for dried food and some fridges for fresh produce. It was a bit cramped but the volunteers all got along well and there was always a buzz of happy chatter as people got to know each other. This is the heart of community as people come together to do good for others and I believe that there is something the church can learn about just getting on and being good news for others rather than spending all our time just telling people about good news.

Everything was running smoothly until March 2020 when, as most people know, the world was stopped by the global Covid pandemic. On 23 March the Prime Minister announced the first

UK-wide lockdown in order to try and contain the spread of the virus and the following day the Archbishop of Canterbury instructed all clergy to close the churches under their care. This was a total ban intended to set an example to the nation that the Church was taking the pandemic seriously. This included not allowing churches to be used for any form of service or for private prayer; even clergy were not allowed to enter their churches to pray on their own. The Archbishop took the lead in this initiative by presiding at a Eucharist on his own from the kitchen of Lambeth Palace which was live streamed for anyone to watch.

This was a massive blow to the lunch project and would have serious consequences for the many vulnerable folk who had come to rely on us to provide them with food; they would also be disproportionately affected by the national shutdown that would limit access to shops and other sources of food provision. I called the Real Junk Food chef to see what we could do to help, what he was willing to do, and how we might organize ourselves. The email to all clergy from the Archbishop included a few lines about allowing foodbanks operating from churches to continue but our project was not a foodbank and was considerably more complicated as it involved cooking and all the preparation necessary when dealing with fresh food. The chef agreed we should do something and was willing to step up and so I set about contacting the Archbishop, my Archdeacon and the Brighton and Hove Council environmental health department to get advice.

I got an amazingly quick response from environmental health saying that what we provided was a vital service and we should continue, no matter what the Archbishop said, and sending me some guidance they had already drafted. The Archdeacon responded similarly and thanked me for this enormously important work which he thought was fantastic. I never got a response from Lambeth Palace but I guess they were a bit busy with other things and didn't have any time to worry about an eccentric little church in Brighton looking to defy their rules for the good of those in need.

We decided that we would move the food preparation into the main body of the church – after all, we weren't allowed to hold any services there and moving into this large space would allow a small number of volunteers to really distance themselves from each other, reducing the risk of passing the virus around. We limited the number of volunteers to six and the chef was the only person allowed in the kitchen. Everyone had to wear facemasks at all times and I also sourced some full-face visors for people to wear in addition to a mask if they wanted to. Clinical gloves were supplied for everyone to limit the risk of infection through contact and everyone who was happy to volunteer agreed to test for Covid on a weekly basis. By the end of that first week of lockdown we had a plan, had written guidance about how we were going to operate which had been approved by environmental health, and posted a notice on the church doors informing people that we would be offering a hot takeaway meal from the front door.

I've never been too worried about breaking rules which I feel are unjust or unnecessary and to some extent feel that this is one of the things we're called to do as Christians when we're confronted with injustice. Jesus often questioned authority and the established order, especially when the systems in place disadvantaged those who were least well off in society, and it felt quite Christ-like to be defying the authority of the Archbishop in order to serve those in need. I was tickled by the absurdity that every Tuesday and Wednesday the church was a hive of socially distanced activity but every other day of the week, even Sundays, I wasn't even allowed to go into church on my own to pray!

A few weeks later, while the rest of the country was mostly locked indoors apart from being allowed to go out for an hour for a socially distanced walk, we opened for our first takeaway service. A queue soon formed outside the church as a number of our regular customers arrived to collect a compostable container full of steaming hot food which they took back to their home to consume. I donned my facemask, hat and gloves so that I could patrol outside the church, ensuring that people stayed 2m apart and didn't stick around to eat their meal as that would encourage others to stay and start congregating in non-compliance with the lockdown rules. After a few days the news got out about what we were doing and the queue got longer, snaking down the road and round the corner. I bought a can of spray chalk and crafted a stencil from some foam board with a cut-out of two footprints and the legend '2m' cut into it and graffitied this simple sign every 2 metres along the church wall to encourage people to keep their distance. Traces of these symbols of the pandemic exist to this day embedded deep in the cracks and crevices of the brickwork of our old Victorian wall.

Alongside this I put out a call for volunteers who would be prepared to help their neighbours in any way as long as it stayed within the lockdown rules. Within a week I had a list of 70 volunteers who were prepared to do shopping for someone, deliver medication, check on isolated neighbours and help distribute the lunches to people who couldn't come out to collect the food themselves. Quite quickly we began to come across stories of peculiar tastes and behaviour as well as evidence of difficulty and stress. We discovered one person who was extremely picky about the food being delivered and who sometimes wanted to send it back even though we tried our best to stick to their rigid requirements. After a while the requests for food became a little erratic and we realized that they were accessing a variety of services offering meals and making a selection based on the menu on offer each day. Another person asked me for a referral to the foodbank and I arranged for a regular pickup for them. One day when there was no-one available to collect their food parcel, the recipient assured me it was OK as they had paid for a taxi to go and collect it for them, which made me wonder if the taxi fare couldn't have been better used to buy food!

What I did learn is that these requests are not unreasonable. Many people are incredibly grateful to receive whatever help we're able to provide, but just because they are in a position of needing to rely on handouts doesn't mean that our provision should be sub-standard. Everyone deserves to be treated with respect, in the same way and to the same standard, and it was right for people to expect the same level of service and courtesy as I would. Jesus talked about this in a discourse about judgement and hypocrisy in Matthew 7 when he concluded 'in everything do to others what you would have them do to you'. This is one of the reasons I don't accept second-hand clothing to pass on to those who come to our various drop-ins: the clothes are usually being thrown out because they're worn out or unusable by the donor. I have the same rule about jumble sales following an early sale at my church where I was horrified to see a whole clothes rail full of old bras which someone thought would be an attractive purchase! I'd rather take someone to the shops and give them the money to buy underwear than expect anyone to put up with second-hand lingerie!

The other thing I learned is how many amazing volunteers there are who are prepared to give so much of their time and energy to help those in need. That experience of coming together during lockdown to keep a food provision going has resulted in an ongoing service that has expanded and grown. We still open every Tuesday and Wednesday, feeding around 100 people every day. But this service isn't just about feeding people. The environment created by the volunteers is welcoming and sociable and the people who turn up are there as much for the social contact as they are for the food. For many of them this is the only time they get to see others and chat to them and it's wonderful to see the mix of generations and backgrounds present at every lunch.

We now have a community of volunteers who not only come together to prepare food and serve those who come to eat, but also look out for the wider needs of those who come to us in need. I'm often asked by one volunteer or another if I can sit down with a particular person who seems especially troubled that day, or I'm pointed towards someone who is particularly vulnerable and needs some help with housing or benefits or their mental health. These are good-hearted folk looking out for the needs of the whole person who comes to us for food but goes away with so much more. This is most evident at Christmas when the volunteers not only decorate the church and serve the most amazing Christmas dinner, but they also put their hands into their own pockets to buy gifts for everyone who comes to the lunch so that no-one goes away empty handed. Toiletries, chocolates, cakes and useful gifts such as vacuum flasks or torches are all handed out with generosity and joy.

During lockdown the theological thinktank Theos produced a report as part of its GRA:CE project entitled 'Growing Good: Growth, Social Action and Discipleship in the Church of England'.[1] This was the culmination of three years' research commissioned by the Church Urban Fund into the relationship between church social action, volunteering and church attendance and proposed that we should focus on those who take part in social action work in church buildings as primary places for invitation to engage more deeply with Christian faith. Following this the Church Urban Fund developed an excellent small group study course called the Growing Good Toolkit and we were happy to pilot this at St Luke's, running a weekly small group for six weeks and at the same time theming the concurrent Sundays with the same material. It's a fabulous course for churches who want to engage with social action and help their volunteers and congregation in their journey of faith, and it's free.[2]

This has helped us to understand the motivation of some of those who volunteer at all our midweek projects and inspired us to find ways to connect the wonderful people who give so freely of their time with the faith life of St Luke's. We've begun to hold special Sunday services when we focus on one particular project and invite the volunteers to come along so that we can celebrate their work and pray for them. We've had a Real Junk Food Sunday which coincided with harvest festival, we've had Newnote Sunday featuring music from the recovery orchestra and guitar group as well as carol services highlighting the various community choirs that use the building.

The accounts of the last supper that Jesus held with his disciples include the preparation for this meal as well as the conversations that took place during it. Jesus gave that meal divine significance through his words and actions and I believe that our preparation and provision of food for anyone who wants it is following in the footsteps of this divine act. I'm not sure providing corned beef hash to a hundred hungry souls is a sacramental act but it does do more than just feed their bodies. We've recently extended our food ministry into development of an after-school cooking club where 7–11 year-olds come to spend an hour cooking a meal and learning about nutrition. When the meal is ready their families come to the church and everyone gets to sit and eat a wonderful healthy meal. The buzz of happy families eating and chatting together at supper and the pride of the youngsters who want to show their parents the food they've prepared feels pretty divine to me and more than makes up for the first aid necessary the first time we did this and asked the children to peel potatoes! We learned from that experience to pre-prepare anything that might need a knife and I believe that the care that we show these children and those who come to eat helps them to feel the presence of God as they share with each other and break bread together.

Notes

1 https://www.theosthinktank.co.uk/research/2000/01/31/the-grace-project
2 https://growing-good.org.uk/

7

Music as Balm to the Soul

I don't know if this is a gospel value (if there is such a thing) but I try to have a policy of saying yes to anyone who approaches me with an idea, especially if it's about using the church building for good. This has got me into trouble a few times but it's also provided amazing opportunities. One such opportunity landed on my doorstep when a parishioner asked to see me about an idea she'd had. She was a TV producer and had just finished a one-off documentary about music and addiction which had transformed her life and spawned an idea. Addicts Symphony featured ten classical musicians who had suffered from addiction and followed their progress as they worked towards a performance with the London Symphony Orchestra. The programme charted the support they were able to give each other, the highs and lows of pressurized classical rehearsals and the heartwarming stories of the individuals and their past lives and aspirations for the future.

The programme turned out to be a transformative experience not just for the participants but also for some of the production team and that was what prompted the producer to approach me. She had decided that she wanted to dedicate herself to this kind of work and had an idea to use the basic premise to set up a project supporting addicts through music. The drawback was that she had no idea how to do this or where to start and for some reason she thought her local vicar might be able to help! I could see it was a great idea and knew that some of the people who were coming to our drop-in meals were also addicts or in recovery and might benefit from something like this. As a local church I wanted to help as much as I could but we had no money to kickstart a project like this. What we did have was a building so I offered to let her use the church one evening a week for free to help get this project off the ground. I gave the now former TV producer a set of keys and waited to see what would happen.

Within months I began to hear strange sounds coming from the church next door to my vicarage and could see that the lights were on and people were going in and out. After a while I thought I'd pop in to see what was going on and was greeted with a church full of people and the strangest collection of instruments I'd ever seen. There seemed to be a lot of percussionists and guitar players, a couple of keyboardists, a flautist, some singers and someone with a massive tuba. They were spread all over the church in a seemingly random arrangement but all very chatty and cheerful and the level of noise was mostly coming from their conversation and discussion. Occasionally they actually played together and I wondered where they had managed to find compositions which catered for such an unusual mix of instruments but realized once they started that they weren't following any set music, but improvising under the direction of a conductor who expertly guided them to create music that made the best use of the assortment of musical talent that littered the room. I subsequently discovered that not all of them could read music anyway so improvisation was the key tool in helping them to create music together.

As this project developed the most impressive thing was the friendships that were being established. The road to recovery is all about mutual support from others on the same journey, and bringing together a group of music-loving individuals was a brilliant way to make this possible without the single-minded focus on addiction that you get from an Alcoholics Anonymous group, although being involved in AA is also an important part of any addict's journey. Playing music together is a wonderful way to create a sense of community, especially when improvisation is the core technique of the group because this requires collaboration and listening to each other. It also took account of the varying skills of the people in the room and allowed everyone to take part in the way that was most appropriate to them.

There was a slight problem that I hadn't anticipated, which

MUSIC AS BALM TO THE SOUL

was largely a function of the unusual composition of the orchestra. Having so many percussionists meant that the music being played was often quite loud, especially when added to by those with electric guitars who needed to turn their volume up so they could hear above the noise of the drummers right next to them. Early one evening my doorbell went and I was confronted by an angry neighbour who wanted me to know that the racket from the church was unbearable, especially as he worked from home and his office was at the back of the house facing the church. This was not the first time I'd had a complaint from this neighbour, who seemed to be unaware that music was an integral part of church life and that there were likely to be many occasions when there was noise of one sort or another coming from this building. I tried to comfort him by saying that all music would stop by 10pm but that if he found it intolerable, he was welcome to write to the council with a complaint. I felt confident about the consequences of any formal process with the council because the head of environmental health at the council, which is the department that deals with noise complaints, was a member of my PCC and had already given me advice about any sound emanating from the building that someone might consider a nuisance.

It's one of the problems and joys of having a church building that is integrated so closely with the community. St Luke's is nestled among closely-packed terraced houses with small gardens that were mostly built after the church. There's a wonderful map in Brighton Museum of the area in 1875 which shows the church and some streets to the south and east of its current location, but nothing to the north or west. Originally the building must have sat in glorious isolation looking out over fields that stretched up to the Sussex Downs in one direction and with panoramic views of the sea in the other. My defence to those who complain about any noise coming from the church is that we were here first and that any house owner must have seen there was a church nearby when they purchased their home and therefore should expect some level of noise occasionally.

It turned out that this particular resident had a historical beef with the church about noise because a previous incumbent had been a fan of high-octane worship songs and had the benefit of a worship band who liked to crank up the volume of their contributions on Sunday morning to a deafening level, perhaps hoping that the neighbours would be inspired to worship God in their homes when they heard the strains of the latest worship song played on guitar amps turned up to eleven. I discovered this when a letter was posted through my door one day which turned out to be a copy of a complaint made five years before I even became the vicar, containing similar gripes about the noise emanating from our premises. It made me realize that the relationship between the church and its parish always predates the present incumbent and that this is a factor that we need to take into account in our ministry. We are always temporary tenants of the role and the neighbourhood in which we're placed and there will always be residents and congregation members who have a much stronger claim to the church than we do as mere fly-by-nights.

The temporary nature of our ministry in place is exacerbated by the fact that these days so many priests move on after five years, despite the fact that research shows that growth and meaningful ministry only starts to take place once someone has been in post for at least seven years. The more recent strategy of placing people in three-year interim posts or giving central church grants for projects to turn around a church in three to five years also goes against any meaningful long-term planning. The glory of the Church of England is the parish system and the way it ensures that every square inch of the country is ministered to by someone who lives locally and understands the particularity of the neighbourhood in which they're placed. I would suggest that this dedication to geography should also extend to longevity of service and that the church should be investing in more long-term placement of those in ministry. I know there is enormous value in the fact that I now know teenagers and their families that I first got to meet when they came to our parent/toddler group, or that there are staff working in the local pub who remember me from school assemblies and the Jesus bag I always use to carry my props in. It takes time to build this kind of relationship and shows a commitment to the community that is all too often absent from agencies, social projects and other forms of community professionals who live with the pain of short-term funding and frequent changes of policy. Even our MPs only get to be in post for five years before another election comes along and the possibility of a change. The Church could and should offer a more lasting relationship between pastor and parish if it has the resources to commit to that.

I was happy to live with the racket coming from the church, knowing that there was a far more important objective being accomplished. People were being transformed from destitution and dependence on alcohol or drugs to become creative members of society, contributing artistically and positively to the richness of the culture of the city. Along the way they were being supportive of others on the same journey and were removing a burden from social services and the NHS by becoming responsible, healthy members of society. This fitted with my understanding that Jesus brought transformation, healing and wholeness to so many around him and asked us to do the same. It doesn't matter to me that the people leading this project don't attribute this work to God, although there is a strong emphasis in the recovery community of reliance on a higher power. As far as I'm concerned, they are doing the work of the Kingdom and God is in it and working through it and blessing it.

The project grew and became established and felt like a really good fit alongside other recovery initiatives that were developing at the church. Around the same time, I was approached by someone who wanted to set up what he called a recovery prayer group and once again I exercised my ministry of affirmation and simply said yes. Within weeks a Monday night, step eleven, alcoholics anonymous group was up and running and is still running today with anything up to 50 attendees for an hour of support and fellowship. The most important part of this is 20 minutes of full silence, one of the most beautiful, holy and spiritual things that happens in the church each week. I now understand that this is part of the practice of a step eleven group that encourages people to connect with their higher power during this time of quiet. The leaders of the group that meets in my church are very happy to explicitly talk about this as a time of prayer and refer to God as the object of this meditative hour. There is something deeply spiritual about sitting in a church with 50 strangers in complete silence. I can understand why the Quakers place such high value on corporate silence and I occasionally drop in on the Monday group for a spiritual top-up of my own. This feels like the opposite of the noisy, animated energy of the Tuesday recovery orchestra and I'm glad we're able to host both extremes.

The music project grew in popularity and began to receive funding from the Arts Council and various other grant-making bodies and was producing really interesting music. It became clear, however, that there were some who wanted to take part but who didn't have the skill or confidence to join in wholeheartedly with the improvisation. Most of these were guitarists and so the idea formed of setting up a second group just to play guitar with an emphasis on strumming away to fairly well-known songs such as 'Sweet Caroline' or 'House of the Rising Sun'. So a Friday morning 'strummers' group was set up for those with basic guitar skills or who wanted a bit of a singalong. This seemed to attract a slightly different clientele to the orchestra, consisting of some people who were a bit more vulnerable than the Tuesday night attendees, and so was clearly meeting a different need. But one of the difficulties was that they didn't always have their own guitar or were unable to lug a heavy electric guitar and amp across the city to our church for the sessions.

The organizers decided to approach a guitar company to see if they could help but they forgot to tell me! The first I knew of this was when a courier knocked on my door to ask what I wanted to do with the guitars. It turned out he had four brand new Fender electric guitars for my attention, all beautifully boxed up direct from the manufacturer, and wanted me to sign for them! I thought at first that someone wanted to treat me and was encouraging me to get back to playing the guitar, which I had been so keen on as a teenager. I wasn't going to turn down such a generous gift so I signed the delivery note and brought the precious instruments into my study. It was only on looking at the label that I realised these were not for me but for the orchestra, which I was quite relieved about as my fingers are nowhere near nimble enough to manage guitar chords anymore. This turned out to be just the beginning as for the rest of the week I answered the door to more couriers with Fender amps, guitar stands, cases, leads and packets of strings – everything you would ever need to set up a rock band with top notch gear. Someone had done a great job in persuading Fender of the worthiness of this recovery project and they had responded really generously; it was wonderful and gave the strummers group a real boost.

As the two groups became more established, they started to put on occasional concerts and were invited to take part in various events, both musical and recovery themed. These started by using the church building as the venue and we had some raucous nights with the orchestra, some of the strummers and a local recovery choir playing a wide variety of types of music, always finishing by 10pm so as not to annoy the neighbours. World-famous bass player Herbie Flowers turned up for some of the gigs, complete with double bass and a whole evening full of stories of working with Lou Reed on 'Walk on the Wild Side' and many other famous artists including David Bowie, Marc Bolan and Elton John. My memory of him was that he seemed to spend more time telling stories than playing music as he was a great raconteur and will be sadly missed. Slowly the fame and reputation of the charity spread as they received awards for excellence, music composition, and recently a King's award for voluntary service.

Alongside these achievements there were also sad times, as not everyone was able to persist in their recovery journey and I found myself being asked if it was possible to use the church so that people could come together to remember a friend who had died. This was another opportunity to say yes and I hosted a number of gatherings for musicians who had unfortunately lost their way and lost their lives to the damaging effects of alcohol or drugs. No-one would describe these impromptu, and usually improvised, events as a memorial service or a gig, but because there were a lot of musicians in the room inevitably someone would feel the need to get their guitar out and sing and others would join in and we'd be treated to an impromptu evening of music and improvisation as well as heartfelt stories about the person who'd died and some of their past exploits in the music business.

These were amazingly spiritual occasions when the recovery community's understanding of a higher power meshed with my Christian faith and the baked-in holiness of a church building. I was often oblivious to the fame of some of the musicians who would turn up from all over the country or make a deviation from their current touring schedule so that they could be in Brighton to honour their departed friend. It gave people a chance to sing the songs that they used to play together and share in the odd reunion that the death of someone close often instigates. I loved to see the church full of rock musicians with the smell of cigarette smoke hanging heavy in the air just outside the front door and the clink of bottles being passed around in memory of the departed. It was a privilege to host these occasions and I always felt blessed as I said a few words about our mortality and our relationship to eternity and blessed the assembled company in the name of the Father and the Son and the Holy Spirit.

It seemed an obvious thing to ask the orchestra and guitar group to come on a Sunday and contribute musically to our worship and so I broached the idea with the founder. Due to the nature of the music produced by the orchestra and the makeup of the ensemble we agreed that their 20 or 30-minute piece of improvisation wouldn't really fit within the format or a normal Sunday morning service or be appropriate for a congregation used to singing hymns and contemporary worship songs. But we thought the strummers would be able to contribute as their music was mostly singalong songs anyway; we'd just need to adjust it to include worship songs. We decided the easiest format for bringing these together was in a carol service and so I left them to rehearse and tell me which carols they would like to play.

The day of the carol service came and the guitar group turned up mid-afternoon to rehearse and it was then that I began to wonder whether this was a good idea. As the group were all fairly new to playing guitar the music arrangements had to be very simple and in keys that work for a guitarist which are not necessarily the same keys that are conducive to congregational singing. Added to that was the 'strident' way in which the guitars were played. To get eight novice instrumentalists to stay in time with each other it was important to keep a nice, steady beat and so they would all strum their guitars in synchronization with each other, resulting in a 'twang' 'twang' 'twang' 'twang' with a very heavy beat and often quite forceful strumming. While this was okay for 'Hark The Herald Angels Sing' it wasn't so great for 'Away in a Manger' or 'Silent Night' which both had a tinge of heavy metal to the accompaniment. Added to this was the fact that sometimes chord changes caused a pause in the rhythm of the song due to the complicated fingering that was required for the next chord. So we would get 'O Come All Ye *pause pause pause* Faithful *pause pause pause*, Joyful and Tri *pause pause* umphant'. Nevertheless, the evening went really well and the strummers were full of pride at what they'd been able to achieve.

More recently I was privileged to attend a packed-out event at the Royal Opera House in Covent Garden to see this rag-tag group of former addicts perform along with a recovery dance group to a rapturous reception. This kind of transformation from distress and despair to a place of honour, value and achievement seems to me to be the kind of journey God wants everyone to make and which we should be facilitating in our churches.

8

Church and Community

What does it mean to be a parish church? Does parish mean anything these days when people are so mobile and the boundaries often created for parishes centuries ago don't seem to make sense to the community that has grown up in the meantime? There is a particular challenge for churches set in an urban environment when there are often many churches within quite a small area and so churchgoers can indulge in a little church shopping when it comes to choosing the building they worship in on Sunday, if that's even part of their daily life.

The church I serve is close enough to the centre of Brighton to be considered a city centre church, but far enough away from the urban hub of shops, clubs and pubs to be a comfortable residential area. With a couple of excellent state infant and junior schools nearby and being only ten minutes' walk from Brighton station with its easy access to London, it's a fantastic place for commuters to live, so house prices reflect the relative affluence of the residents and the demographic is very middle class.

The faith mix is interesting because the 2021 census shows that only just over 20 per cent of the residents in the parish regard themselves as Christian; this is less than half of the national average. Conversely, over 60 per cent consider themselves to have no religion, compared with a national figure of just over 35 per cent. What relevance does church have to its community in this set of circumstances? What does it mean to be the holder of the 'cure of souls' of a geographic area when a majority of the people who live there don't believe they have a soul? For me it means getting involved in the things that people in my parish care about and showing that these are things that God cares about as well, even when at first sight it has nothing to do with faith at all.

My initiation into community involvement began when plans were announced to redevelop a local road junction where seven roads met at one of the most poorly designed mini-roundabouts I had ever seen. It consisted of a pitiful circle of paving stones covered in traffic signs that stood in the middle of a maelstrom of traffic fighting its way around two lanes of tarmac, hemmed in by metal safety barriers that made the whole environment feel like a prison. There were constant accidents as cars, trucks and buses scraped into each other as they sped around the mess trying to work out which lane to get into so that they could get to the exit they wanted. Cyclists were in constant peril and were frequently knocked over, and I sometimes watched in horror as the lay reader of the church wobbled slowly round this storm of vehicles on a rickety old bike, steering with one hand and holding the lead of his dog in the other which obediently trotted along beside him. A grant had been obtained to completely redesign the junction and a call was put out for locals to join a small consultation group to help represent the views of the community as this scheme progressed.

As a local community leader, I volunteered to join the group and offered the church as a suitable meeting space as it was close to the junction in question. I soon found myself in a meeting with a dozen or so residents listening to the project leaders and some members of the design team and the council outline their plans for the junction. These included expanding the mini-roundabout to make it much bigger thereby reducing the lanes around it from two to one, landscaping the centre of the roundabout and removing all the barriers that were supposed to protect pedestrians. The project manager explained that they had monitored the junction for some time and discovered that quite a few pedestrians were frustrated with the barriers and often jumped over them to get across the junction quicker but were then trapped between the traffic and the unyielding barricade, sometimes resulting in crushing injuries. The reduced lanes would make it clearer to drivers how to navigate around and these would also have some runoff space beside them that would act as safe havens for cyclists.

The plans seemed to me to be well thought out and there had clearly already been a considerable amount of work done to get to this point. I thought it would all be plain sailing from then on – how wrong could I be! The first person to speak once the plans had been explained was very forthright and told us all that his only reason for being in the group was to make sure nothing was changed and, in particular, he violently opposed any plans to remove the railings. This set a tone of dissent that the whole group picked up on and the rest of the meeting was filled with statements of dissatisfaction about everything from the reduction of the lanes from two to one to the sketch of the landscaping of the central reservation. People didn't like the idea that getting from one side of the junction to the other might involve a few extra metres walking and there was major concern that reducing traffic at the junction would result in an increase in cars using local side streets. It turns out people don't mind seeing improvements to facilities nearby as long as it doesn't affect their own road, especially if that might impact the parking!

I felt the design team handled everything very patiently and professionally and assured them of my positive support once everyone had gone and we packed up tables and chairs after the meeting. We made plans for a series of public exhibitions of the plans in the church, which would go along with a major leaflet drop in the area and information in the local press about the project. Over the coming months things progressed quite quickly, there were a few minor changes to the design following public feedback and dates were set for the work to commence; everything appeared to be going smoothly until a major problem raised its head.

Sitting beside one of the roads into the junction was a large, mature elm tree. Brighton is proud to host the National Elm Tree Collection because it was one of the few areas not affected by the epidemic of elm disease that decimated trees across the UK in the 1970s and there are many majestic elm trees all over the city. As the design included reformatting pavements around the junction and widening some roads, this meant that the Seven Dials elm was due to be removed. Quite late on in the consultation process it began to be clear that people were very concerned about this. Myself and other members of a local community association worked with the design team to come up with some creative solutions to help allay any concerns. These included a local sculptor who offered to carve a section of the elm tree trunk to create a bench in the same location as the tree and some of the wood being used to create a cross to be installed in the church.

Tree conservation is a very emotive topic and I got wind of an alternative public meeting that had been set up to discuss this issue. I went along, slightly fearful as I had been a public advocate for the development in its entirety, and found quite an angry group packed into a local community hall intent on stopping the removal of the tree no matter what. This was followed shortly afterwards by a series of protests to protect the tree culminating in some people climbing into it, determined to stay put until the threat of removal was removed. The protest made national headlines with the Daily Mail dubbing it 'A very middle-class protest: Residents occupy 170-year-old elm tree after Green Party council threaten to chop it down'.

Much to my surprise the protests worked and the council instructed the contractors and project team to find a way to redesign that junction so that the tree could be retained. Even more of a surprise was how easy this was for them to do and the work proceeded with hardly any delay in the overall timescale. Following six months of construction, road closures, traffic management schemes and project updates, everything was coming close to a conclusion. We were approaching Christmas and I could see an opportunity to do a community event to mark the completion of the work which would also help to smooth over any of the discord that had arisen during the consultation, protest and discussion around this initiative. I contacted the project team and proposed a Christmas carol singing evening that would incorporate a 'Blessing of the Roundabout'. They responded really positively and even said they could give us a small budget so I set about organizing an evening the week before Christmas.

As the junction marked the boundary between two parishes, I contacted the neighbouring priest who was considerably more traditional than I, to ask if he would like to be involved. He responded positively and offered the church choir to take part and we agreed to combine this with a community choir that met at St Luke's to help lead the singing of Christmas carols. At the same time I contacted a friend of mine whose church possessed a set of stand-alone nativity figures that were about two thirds life-size. He agreed to loan them to me and I made arrangements with the council to install them on the new roundabout, suitably chained together so that they couldn't be blown into the traffic by the winter winds.

The night of the blessing arrived and so did the most humungous December storm. The rain lashed down from early in the morning and showed no signs of abating for the evening event. Fortunately, an estate agent had their offices directly looking onto the junction and they kindly agreed to open for the evening so that we could celebrate in the dry and pretty soon the showroom was packed with people drinking mulled wine, singing carols at the top of their voices and patting each other on the back at the completion of this major project. At the midpoint of the evening, I asked for some hush and gave a little speech thanking all those who had been involved and expressing my hope that this development would help to improve our neighbourhood. Then the priest from the neighbouring parish, dressed head to toe in black including a very impressive cloak and a biretta perched on his head, ventured out into the pouring rain to stand in the middle of the roundabout and ask for God's blessing on this new scheme. He sprinkled holy water on the holy family installed around a tree lit up with Christmas lights while God poured his blessing on the site with water from heaven.

The nativity stayed in place for the following week although one of the lambs mysteriously disappeared one night only to reappear on social media in various different settings thanks to the poor beasts' abductors. The 'lost' sheep looked like it was having quite a lot of fun and didn't want to be found by any good shepherds that happened to be searching and seeking for the lost. After Midnight Mass on Christmas Eve, I crept out to the nativity scene and placed a baby doll in the manger as a sign that Jesus was present in our neighbourhood that Christmas morning. Over the following days I found him propped up in various poses in his makeshift bed along with little gifts left by passers-by who appreciated the presence of the Son of God at this wonderful time of year.

This whole roundabout redesign took just over a year but was not the only introduction I had to community politics. There were at least two other major neighbourhood issues to protest about, prompting me to write a piece in our local community magazine about the propensity for our residents to kick up a stink.

Article in the Prestonville Friend Magazine April 2013

The Revolting People of Prestonville

The last few months has seen the rise of a whole variety of community action groups in our area, voicing their concerns about issues that are important to us all. The church has been happy to act as a venue for a number of these concerns so I've seen and heard at first-hand how passionate people can get when our community life is threatened by change.

It began in January with the news that the field we all know as BHASVIC field was to be fenced in by Cardinal Newman School as a result of concerns about safeguarding and health and safety of the children who use it. Friends of the Field was set up and have just recently lodged an application for the field to be given Village Green status so that it can remain in public use as well as being the playing field for the schools in our area.

This was closely followed by news of a proposal for the Anston House site between Dyke Road Drive and Preston Park with plans for a 15-storey block to be built which would shadow part of the park and many of the houses backing onto it. These plans have currently been withdrawn while the developers re-visit some of their data but will come back to the council sometime soon, so keep an eye out for more news about this.

Most recently we've had the protests about the removal of a large elm tree as part of the Seven Dials redevelopment including a couple of days of tree sitting by two determined protesters. Discussions about this are ongoing and will be debated by the council at one of their meetings in April.

Although most of these activities could be described as community protest, they have been largely characterized by good natured positivity and my hope is that they will continue in this vein.

Alongside all of this the church is hoping to inject some purely celebratory activities this springtime as we launch our first ever Spring Fair on 20th April followed shortly after by the visit of the Bishop of Chichester to St Luke's to re-license myself as Vicar of the parish of Prestonville on 1st May. This has come about because the parish has itself been under the threat of reorganization for the last dozen or so years, but that uncertainty has been lifted and I can now take up the formal title of Vicar rather than Priest-in-Charge. I hope you will be able to join us for these celebrations of the life of this amazingly active community and that the church will continue to be an important part of that.

I firmly believe that involvement in these kinds of campaigns helped our church to re-establish its position as the parish church of the area. Too often churches come to be seen as the domain of the few who attend it and becomes restricted to a 'Sunday only' mentality. This can be especially true in an urban setting when a resident can pick and choose the church style that suits them rather than go to the church most local to them. It may be that your taste is for happy, clappy church but your parish church only does smells and bells, while two parishes across is just the kind of church for you and it's only another ten minutes to walk. This was the case with St Luke's, which was known for being one of the few charismatic evangelical Anglican churches in central Brighton and so attracted a congregation from all over the city with a group of people with little or no connection to the geographic parish. Getting stuck into local community concerns helped to re-establish the status of St Luke's as a church concerned about its parish.

The next community concern came about because of a dispute which turned into a proper strike. Not a dispute with us but an argument between the refuse collection service and the council. There's no better time to have a bin strike than the summer at the seaside when the city is busy with holidaymakers and the temperatures, both physical and emotional, get raised. What's that got to do with the church, you may ask? Unfortunately, it does concern us because St Luke's is situated on a street corner where a series of communal refuse bins are located. These are a constant problem even in peaceful times because non-typical items tend to get dumped alongside these bins and the most convenient place is on the thin sliver of land that runs around the church. Mattresses, beds, sofas, bookcases, books, toys and old records all get shoved onto our land if they can't be made to fit into the bins or people can't be bothered to open the lid.

When there's a strike this becomes a serious public health hazard as well as causing a lot of inconvenience to local residents. One particular period of industrial action lasted over a month and rubbish build-up around the communal refuse bins began to get quite serious. The pavement became blocked, plastic bags of rotting food and used nappies started to spill their contents, while seagulls helped the process along by picking open anything they thought might contain food and strewing it all over the road. Very quickly the corner of the street overlooked by the church spire began to look a total mess and started to smell and there were reports of mice and rats being seen rooting around the rubbish, competing with the seagulls for any titbit they could find.

I thought I ought to do something about this, not just because I was the vicar but even as a concerned, responsible citizen. I couldn't pick up all the rubbish and get it to the dump, which wasn't open anyway as the workers there were also on strike; what we needed was an alternative receptacle for the refuse. I had a couple of builders' bulk bags in our garden shed and although these were large, they were nowhere near big enough. A bit of internet search yielded the information that there are a whole variety of sizes of these bags and so I promptly ordered one that was the size of a large car and a second one half that size. When they arrived, I put on my gardening gloves, armed myself with a snow shovel and started to transfer the scattered bags of waste from the pavement to the largest bag. After a few hours work the bag was half full with piles of refuse stacked up against the inner wall of the bag so that it stood open ready to receive more rubbish. I prepared a couple of laminated signs and taped them to the communal bins and the new giant binbag, encouraging residents to put their rubbish in the bag rather than on the street and it worked! Over the next few days, the bag began to fill up and I noticed people sometimes picking up stray rubbish and adding it to the bag so that the street remained clean. When the big bag filled up, I added the smaller one and prayed that the strike would end before I had to buy any more.

After a couple of weeks, the strike fortunately ended before I had to start ordering more bags and council workers began to clear the backlog of overflowing bins around the city. When they turned up on our street corner, they noticed my impromptu solution to the rubbish crisis and commended me for my imaginative community spirit. That didn't help in emptying the bag though and I was beginning to worry about how I would get rid of what was now tons of rubbish piled to overflowing along the church wall. Fortunately, the message got back to bin collection head office and I got a call thanking me for this initiative and telling me that a refuse truck had been allocated just to us and would be around shortly to clear everything. Sure enough, a lorry arrived that afternoon along with several workers and they made quick work of transferring everything into the crusher, leaving me with two enormous, fairly pristine bulk bags which I now have in storage in case of another strike.

There were so many positive outcomes from this simple act of community spirit. For months after the strike I was stopped by locals on the street to say how much they appreciated the church stepping up and providing a solution to help keep their streets clean. The clear-up operation initiated a relationship with the refuse and recycling department of the council which has been ongoing ever since because there are always issues with communal recycling bins, fly-tipping and street cleaning. Sadly, it didn't stop people using the church land as an unofficial swap-shop and I still find piles of toys, books, old clothes or bits of furniture that people think someone else might like despite the fact that more often than not everything gets soaked by a rainstorm that makes them unusable. I once picked up a bag of sodden toys and put them in the bin while on my way to a pastoral visit. On my return I found the same bag of toys back on the church land and a note on the vicarage door telling me that these were intended for others to take and I had no right to put them in the bin!

Other community initiatives just come about from the simple policy of saying yes, although the outcomes can be a bit mixed. I like to maintain good relations with the shop owners in our locality and got to know the florist quite well. One autumn he asked me if there was anywhere at the church that he could store Christmas trees in December. I explained that the thin curtain of land around the church wouldn't work because it was open to the public who might be tempted to walk off with a tree or two in the middle of the night, but that the vicarage garden might be a possibility as that was through a locked gate. We had an inspection together and he felt it would work really well so we did a deal that he could store trees in return for a free tree for the church and the vicarage and a small fee.

Towards the end of November, the trees arrived – I had no idea one shop could sell so many! A full-sized articulated lorry arrived and half a dozen helpers began unloading trees and taking them into our back garden. It took all day and by the time they had finished our whole garden was piled head high with over 500 Christmas trees with a small path running through this wall of trees so that it was possible to access everything. Our cat was completely bewildered by this total change to her natural landscape and hid for days and our son took a photograph from his bedroom window and posted it on social media with a quip about his dad being unable to make up his mind about which tree to choose! Throughout December staff from the florists would turn up every day to take a selection of trees to the shop to be sold, churning up our garden as they tramped back and forth and slowly reducing the tree maze as the month progressed. Finally, Christmas came and the last remaining trees were removed leaving behind piles and piles of needles and a garden turned into a sodden mud patch. This was one occasion when saying yes turned out not to be a good idea, although I got to know the florist very well which really helped a few years later when we wanted flowers for my daughter's wedding, and later when he was diagnosed with cancer I was able to give him some pastoral support.

Another garden-related enquiry was much more successful. Most of the odd sliver of land that ran around the southern and eastern borders of the church is laid with hardcore and stone chippings but there was one small section at the eastern end that was an actual garden. A neighbour had asked in the past if she could use this little patch of earth as practice for her permaculture students. I had said yes and some work had gone into making this a small sustainable garden, but the students were only around short-term and permaculture requires long-term attention and the neighbour moved away, so the garden returned to weeds.

A few years later a parishioner approached me about this land. She and a friend were doing a horticulture course but didn't have anywhere to put their learning into practice and they wondered if they could use this little patch of land. I was delighted and said yes, fully expecting another six-month period of activity followed by a loss of interest and the garden returning to wilderness once more. This shows I am a man of little faith because pretty soon this 20m square plot of earth was bursting with tomatoes, potatoes, carrots, chard, spinach and a whole range of herbs. The horticulturalists were incredibly dedicated and were there every week, sometimes every day, weeding, seeding, watering and harvesting and the whole plot looked neat and tidy and began to attract comments of approval from people walking by.

It quickly became clear that these community gardeners meant business and had an appetite for even more. So we began to chat about a larger patch of garden behind the church that was not open to the public but could be accessed through a couple of back doors. I showed them the space, which was four times the size of the street garden, and they began to cook up plans to turn this empty, overgrown patch into a community garden. I gave them some keys and we agreed a couple of work days to clear the plot and create some beds which could be allocated to particular locals who had expressed an interest in getting involved.

My wife got involved and filled one of the beds with tulip bulbs in preparation for the wedding of our daughter, carefully planted so that they would bloom at exactly the right time to be the centrepiece of the floral decorations on her special day.

Within months this barren patch of weeds was transformed into an ordered community garden. The gardeners successfully applied for a grant to allow us to buy a small polytunnel, install a tool shed and build a shelter at one end of the garden so that people could come out and sit and enjoy this little pastoral retreat in the middle of our urban community. I'm amazed that such a small patch of land can produce so much when it's well managed. The community garden is able to provide fresh vegetables and herbs for the community lunches that we produce every week and at harvest time we create little bags of fresh vegetables for the lunch attendees to take home and cook for themselves. We've held open garden events with families coming to see the variety of plants and wildlife now buzzing around this little plot and we've even created a tiny pond in an upturned dustbin lid which is bursting with miniature frogs that we hope will grow to be big enough to help deal with the ongoing battle with slugs. The tulips planted for the wedding burst into life at exactly the right time, adding a welcome splash of colour to the swathes of greenery growing in this burgeoning plot of land.

The community garden has helped us as a church to connect with nature despite being in the middle of a city and has contributed to us attaining an Eco Church Silver award as part of our focus on the environment.

9

Church as a Refuge

Churches are places of sanctuary and for centuries have been recognized as a refuge for those seeking safety. In fact, some parts of the church building are described as the Sanctuary, although you'd be hard pressed to work out which bits of St Luke's Prestonville are sanctified because hardly any of the building would fit the definition of 'being set apart or declared as holy'. We are a truly multi-use building with every bit of the space being used during all the many community activities that take place there every week. Despite our lack of formal Sanctuary we want to be a place of sanctuary because the Bible has a lot to say about the importance of treating the stranger and the foreigner with hospitality and compassion and we wanted to do our bit to help refugees because Brighton had declared itself a city of sanctuary in 2015.

At that time our TV screens were full of footage of The Jungle in Calais. This was a makeshift refugee camp of asylum seekers and migrants all waiting to have their claims for asylum processed or trying to find a way to get across the English Channel to the United Kingdom. Estimates of numbers in the encampment ranged from 3,000 to 10,000 at its height, with people arriving from Somalia, Eritrea, Syria, Afghanistan and many other countries. Conditions there were hideous with no real facilities and frequent violence between different groups. I became aware of a local group that were trying to help and who had put out a call for help from residents of Brighton & Hove and so I got in touch to see if there was some way we could help.

I met the organizers and they told me their biggest need was to find somewhere to act as a collection point and storage for donated items that could be taken over to Calais to help those in need. I showed them the church choir loft which they thought would be an ideal place to sort and store donations ready to be transported to France. We agreed certain days and times during the week when the doors could be open for people to drop off donations and I gave them a set of keys so they could open up and have volunteers on site to manage things. Posts went out on social media to let people know about this arrangement and I left them to get on with the project, feeling pleased that we were doing our bit to help this crisis just across the sea. What I hadn't bargained for was the extraordinary generosity and passion the people of Brighton & Hove had for a good cause like this.

Within a few weeks the whole of the balcony at the back of church was filled front to back and side to side with black bin bags full of donations, piled up to head height and spilling over into the narrow walkways that had been left to allow access. Bags full of old jeans, t-shirts, sweatshirts, blankets, sleeping bags, airbeds and tents were piled in no particular order so no-one had any idea what was where. Boxes of cooking utensils, saucepans and cooking stoves were balanced precariously among the piles of bags, occasionally toppling over with a loud crash and sometimes the tinkle of broken glass. Every day more items would arrive and be put into anonymous bags and thrown up on top of the piles that were already too high to be reached, often going over the top and falling down the back of an enormous mound of black plastic never to be seen again. It was chaos!

I asked to see the organizers so that we could review what was going on and discovered that they were similarly overwhelmed by the amazing response and at a bit of a loss about how to deal with so much stuff. It turned out that their plan for transporting donations to Calais was to run a campervan over on the ferry once a week at the weekend. The trouble was that we were collecting an articulated lorry load of donations every week, far more than a small campervan would hold. Things were coming in so fast that there wasn't any time or space to sort anything and so it became impossible to work out how to distribute the items in a meaningful way even if they did get to France. It didn't make any sense to give a bag of mixed adult and children's clothes to a 20-year-old Eritrean man who needed a pair of shoes, in the hope that there might be some shoes at the bottom of the bag that were the right size. It was also absolutely impossible to have any form of quality control over what was being dumped in church and there was a distinct smell developing as it became clear that not everything was freshly laundered or even dry!

The task of sorting everything out was just too daunting and the news that came back from Calais with those who took trips out there was quite dispiriting. More often than not the items that they took turned out to be inappropriate because the conditions in the camp were changing day by day. At one point we were told that there was a need for fire extinguishers as lots of tents were accidentally catching fire due to cooking stoves falling over or camp fires getting out of control and that the hot weather had made the camp quite dangerous due to the dry conditions. We put a call out for fire extinguishers and loads turned up over the course of the next fortnight. Feeling very pleased that we were going to be providing help for a specific need, the van was loaded up and we waved the driver off. A day later he came back with the news that he'd arrived after five whole days of pouring rain and the camp was ankle deep in mud so they now needed wellies, not fire extinguishers as you'd be hard pushed to start a fire let alone need to put one out! So we put out another call to collect together wellies, then had to sort them into pairs, load them into a van and send them off to France, only to find the weather had changed again and it was freezing cold so now everyone needed coats and hats!

Every now and then the French police would decide to clear a section of the camp, removing tents and destroying or burning them. People there still needed shelter so they needed new tents, but we had a problem finding tents among the piles of bags and once we did and managed to get them loaded into a van and driven over to France, they had managed to sort something else or had moved on. It became a constant game of chasing the need, receiving news that there was a shortage in the camp, followed by a dash to source that particular article, packing it into the van to get it to France only to find that the need had already been addressed. Meanwhile the piles of bags continued to grow on the church balcony and were not being reduced in any way.

I had a crisis meeting with the organizers and we decided that the best way to help those living in the jungle was to stop collecting donations of things and to ask instead that people who were concerned about the situation donated financially. Then the team could go to Calais, see what the immediate need was and go to a supermarket and fill that need by purchasing the appropriate items to meet that need. We closed the doors to more donations and they busied themselves with setting up online donation platforms and the whole operation switched to a cash collection model which was much more responsive to the needs of people in the camp and didn't need piles of stuff being dragged out of the church, packed into vans and trucked across by ferry. This did however leave us with a legacy of a balcony full of bin bags collecting dust or slowly rotting in the damp and cold of the winter, and the congregation started telling me that they were worried about rats and other vermin finding a home among the debris.

After repeated requests to the organizers asking for a solution for all this stuff, they eventually said they'd found an alternative place to store everything and we agreed a date for removal. I arranged volunteers, the organizers arranged volunteers, and we set to throwing bags over the balcony to hopefully be caught by helpers downstairs and transported out to a waiting van. Contents often spilled out from broken bags and we discovered some pretty unsavoury items buried in the depths of the mountains of donations, but it was nothing a broom, dustpan and brush and occasionally a mop couldn't handle. Finally, I could once again see the floor of the choir loft and happily waved the van and its contents goodbye. I think it all got taken to an abandoned nightclub that not long afterwards got demolished and I suspect all these goodwill donations ended up in landfill somewhere.

This experience didn't put me off wanting to help people who have come to this country from other lands to seek a better life and I began to explore opportunities to partner with other organizations to help those seeking asylum. Through one of the congregation I came into touch with Refugee Tales, a group of people who wanted to turn their experiences of visiting one of the detention centres into something positive. They decided to literally walk in solidarity with people who have been detained by staging a pilgrimage each year with activists, writers, asylum seekers and refugees all walking together and sharing their stories. The writers would then take the accounts of those with lived experience of migration and craft them into tales that were published in annual collections of short stories. Their first pilgrimage started in Dover, so often the landing point for small boats coming across the English Channel, and wound its way along the South Downs to Crawley, close to the main Gatwick detention centre.

We had the privilege of hosting some of the walkers in our vicarage for lunch and had a chance to listen to stories of their homelands and their reasons for leaving, their treatment since arriving in the United Kingdom and the years that many of them spent living in limbo while they waited for the authorities to make a decision about whether they could stay here or not. I often talk positively about liminal spaces, thresholds between one thing and another which are commonly fruitful places of imagination, possibility and fresh starts, but asylum seekers are held in perpetual liminal space that is the opposite of that because they are full of uncertainty, insecurity and anxiety. Offering the opportunity of sanctuary, companionship and hospitality can help to make that experience more positive, akin to the Celtic idea of a thin place where the veil between earth and heaven is so thin that it's possible to get glimpses of glory.

I experienced one such thin place with an asylum seeker one Easter morning. I'm lucky to live in Brighton, with all the delights of this vibrant seaside town and of course a beach which is a great place to experience some of the kind of ministry that Jesus conducted as he preached from a boat or barbecued a fish breakfast for his friends. This particular Easter I had plans to baptize two people in the sea at dawn on Easter day. One was a young mum who had recently come to faith after getting drawn into church by the Beach Hut Advent Calendar that you can read about in *Church Beyond Walls*. The other was also a newcomer to Christian faith who felt called to the priesthood and wanted to get baptized and confirmed so that she could begin the process of discernment and training for ministry.

Early in Holy Week a friend got in touch with me to ask if it was possible to add a third person to the baptism party who was an asylum seeker she had met through her visits to the detention centre. He had fled from Iran after being informed that the authorities were about to come and arrest him because they were displeased that he had become a Christian. I thought it would be a wonderful way to affirm his faith and acknowledge the journey he'd been on both spiritual and physical and readily said yes. We had a chat on the phone, agreed my friend would be his Godmother and made arrangements for that coming Sunday.

Easter Day dawned, as it often does in Brighton, grey and cold – but at least it wasn't raining because quite a crowd gathered on the beach in the semi-darkness waiting for the dawn. We never actually saw the sun but knew it had risen because of the time and we started the service while one of the congregation got a small fire going and began barbecuing some fish for the breakfast after the service. The moment came for the baptism and myself, the three candidates and a couple of lifeguards I'd asked to be on hand all descended into the freezing cold April sea. I was wearing a wetsuit under my surplice as was one of the candidates but the others were braving the cold in just shorts and T-shirts. The mum went first, then the presumptive ordinand and finally the asylum seeker, unsure of his future in this country or his status in law, but sure of his faith in Jesus Christ and dedication to a life following him. He lent back into my arms and slipped under the surface of the water with a serene smile of peace on his face before rising back out with a jubilant shout of joy, and both arms raised heavenward in exultation and triumph. Years of trial and uncertainty slipped away as he entered a new life, washed clean by the waters of baptism and hopeful for his future.

Today he has been given settled status, is happily married, and has qualified as a physiotherapist, helping to ease the workload of the overstretched NHS. I'm grateful for people like him who not only manage to escape awful situations in the country of their birth, but want to come here to contribute to society and do their bit to help make others' lives better.

Our experience with refugees and the organizations that seek to support them has shaped my view of how to help those in crisis in other countries and now, whenever someone expresses some concern about the situation in Sudan, or Syria or Gaza, I make sure I have an appropriate aid agency to refer them to so that they can send cash because that's by far the most effective way of helping appropriately rather than raiding your own wardrobe for pairs of jeans you haven't worn for two years and want to get rid of. I also try to find out from those in need what they think would be the best help for them so that we tailor our response to them rather than do what we think they would like.

We put this into practice when Russia invaded Ukraine and I became aware that there already were Ukrainians living in Brighton who wanted to do something to help those who were fleeing the war and found themselves in the city. I was approached by various people about setting up collections of aid to send out to Ukraine which I politely refused but instead sat down with two Ukrainian women and asked them what would be most useful for them. They replied that they just wanted some social space to meet up with friends and any Ukrainians coming to the city. So, we created a Wednesday afternoon cafe for people to drop in, have some cake and a cup of tea and chat about their experiences and get tips from more long-term residents about the help that might be available in the city.

This grew really quickly, with a separate area being used as a craft space for the children that were coming while mums and some dads chatted away in their native language. There was lots of laughter and some occasional tears and it was clear that this was a much-needed space for those who had experienced significant trauma, a place of sanctuary where they could talk about their distress and share their sadness with others in the same situation.

Pretty soon the council became aware of the cafe and started to come along to offer assistance with benefits or housing or connect people with appropriate agencies, and others turned up to help teach English to those newly arrived in the UK. When Ukraine won the Eurovision song contest some of the younger attendees at the cafe asked if they could hold a concert and they took over the church one evening with singing and poetry and dancing, closing with a rousing rendition of the Ukraine national anthem – there was not a dry eye in the house. Gradually the flow of refugees slowed down and those who were here began to get more settled until eventually the original organizers told me that the cafe was no longer needed. For nine months we had been able to offer sanctuary and a safe space that was shaped around the needs of those in distress, and we hadn't had to deal with bags of old clothes or boxes of dirty crockery!

Church offers sanctuary in other ways as well, and I've already written about recovery groups and the way those in addiction can find sanctuary in church. But there are other groups which find that the sacred space of a church building helps them to find respite and peace. We host a male mentoring charity on Thursday nights which started in Brighton and who regard St Luke's as their home. They partner young men who are at risk of going off the rails or have got themselves into trouble somehow with older mentors who guide them through a twelve-week programme helping them to become responsible adults. It seems there is a generation of young men who find it hard to establish their place in society and sometimes don't have appropriate role models to follow and this charity helps to fill that gap.

I admit I sometimes find the group a little challenging. It's not often that I get to spend time in an exclusively male gathering and a church building full of men can feel a little overwhelming with its mix of boisterous humour and testosterone-fuelled energy. I also realized how little they knew about church and church practice when it came round to Easter one year. As mentioned before they meet on Thursday evenings but during Holy Week churches celebrate Maundy Thursday, the night when Jesus held a Passover meal with the disciples and which we now commemorate as the Last Supper. It has become the custom for us at St Luke's to hold a dinner party in the church that combines elements of a Passover meal with some readings of the last supper accounts and the liturgy of Holy Communion. In preparation for this I contacted the Thursday night charity to inform them that we would need to use the church that night and so it wouldn't be available to them as usual. Their response was that it was important for the continuity of their mentoring to be able to meet that particular night and could we move our event to the Wednesday! I had to point out that the clue was in the name and Maundy Thursday had to be on Thursday and that the church liturgical calendar took precedence over any outside organizations who wanted to use the building. Fortunately, they backed down and found an alternative venue for that one night.

At the end of every twelve week 'term' they hold a kind of graduation ceremony where family and friends are invited to come and witness the passage of each young man into responsible adulthood. Each person comes forward with his mentor and they talk about each other and the things that they have appreciated about their journey together over the past weeks. They often describe how they have found a place of peace and safety that has not just been present in the church building but which permeates out to their families, friends and workplaces and frequently the families respond by testifying to the change in the demeanour of the young man they know. The word that is used to describe this process is blessing, a word that is of course very familiar to us in church and I often get the chance to thank the assembled company for their presence in this place of blessing, grateful that they have found sanctuary there.

Sanctuaries are blessed places that bring blessing to those who encounter them. I don't know how it works but I often feel that the very bricks and mortar of the church have absorbed something of the blessing that has gone on in that place over the years. That the very walls of this sacred space are soaked in the prayers, spoken and unspoken, of those who have come here for solace week after week after week. Churches stand as islands of serenity in the midst of busy 21st-century lives and should be as valued for the emptiness and silence as for their liveliness and service in joyous worship and community provision.

CHURCH AS A REFUGE

A friend of mine once put this into words in a post on social media:

I was asked today what my favourite scent/perfume is? I answered, the scent of an old church, steeped in centuries of whispered prayers and desperate confessions, where the air is thick with incense and secrets. It's a fragrance laced with frankincense and myrrh, rising like smoke from the depths of ancient altars, winding its way through the cracks of time. It clings to the walls of the sacristy, it has undertones of wood of the confessional, soaked up with the tears of the penitent – each grain etched with the burden of a thousand unspoken sins, of doubts too heavy to voice.

There's leather in there too, brittle and cracked, the scent of Bibles long forgotten, handled by souls trembling in search of salvation. They open those pages seeking light, but instead, find the void – black and unyielding – the cold indifference of the universe staring back. It is a perfume of despair wrapped in the illusion of hope but with the sweetness of love, an olfactory hymn to the endless search for meaning in a cosmos that offers no answers.

And then, beneath it all, a faint trail of cinnamon and nutmeg lingers – an afterthought, like the last breath of fallen angels, their wings singed and tattered, forever severed from the divine. It fades, slowly, as if slipping from grace itself, longing to return to the pulse of love that once bound them to the heavens, a love that hums in every molecule, in every aching corner of existence.

Victor Martinez

10

Doorstep Discoveries

Living in a vicarage is both a blessing and a curse, and the location of the house is often the factor that determines which of these it is. The vicarage I live in is right next door to the church, although it's not identified as 'The Vicarage', and it always amazes me that some people are surprised to discover that the large detached building adjacent to the church is the home of the vicar. Maybe they don't think that such an impressive house could possibly be owned by a religious organization. The only people who do seem to realize the occupation of the occupier of this house are those in need and the doorbell regularly rings with an enormous variety of requests.

A fair proportion of these are people who are desperate and that was certainly true of one of the first people to come knocking at my door. It was the middle of the day towards the end of a week and I opened the door to find a man in his sixties who looked quite upset. He very simply told me that he was depressed and distraught and the only thing he could think of to help his situation was to kill himself. As someone new to full-time ministry and only having been in the job a few months I was really thrown by this. It had never occurred to me that answering the door could turn into a life-or-death situation and certainly nothing in my theological training prepared me for this, even though we had done a module on counselling. I knew enough to be able to see that this was a genuine cry for help and that it was important to listen so I invited him in, made us both some tea and we sat down to chat.

Over the next hour I listened to his life story, saying very little myself apart from the odd question prompting him for more detail. He was clearly isolated and alone and having space to talk seemed to be working and his mood lightened as the time went on. Eventually I began to feel that he was more stable emotionally than when we first met and our conversation began to wind down. I asked how he was feeling and what his thoughts were about ending it all now, and he affirmed that he was feeling more positive. I took some contact details from him and let him know that I would do a bit of research about ways we might be able to help him and would contact him in a few days to see how he was getting along.

I called one of our parishioners who I knew to be wise and who had some experience with people in this kind of situation and we agreed to chat after the service on the following Sunday which was only two days away. To my surprise, my doorstep visitor turned up at church on Sunday morning and took part in the service, which he seemed to enjoy. Afterwards I introduced him to the wise parishioner and could see them deep in conversation for quite some time as the rest of the church members milled around drinking coffee and chatting. As things began to quieten down, I saw the two of them leaving together and I went over to say goodbye and discovered that my doorstep visitor had been invited back for a family Sunday lunch.

This began a supportive friendship between the two of them. The visitor on the doorstep became a regular worshipper on Sunday mornings and began coming to our monthly Sunday afternoon drop-in for a meal and after a while started to volunteer to help with washing up. During the week he got involved as a volunteer in a community farming project which was run by another church but included volunteers from our church. It turned out he had been a butcher earlier in his life and his skills were soon put to use on the farm preparing meat. They eventually offered him a home along with two or three other volunteers in a house on the farm that was much better accommodation for him and also meant he had company rather than being isolated in a flat on his own. The congregation member continued to keep in touch with him, offering advice and support as appropriate and keeping me informed of his progress. This continued for a number of years until ill health brought about its own decline and he eventually passed away naturally and peacefully in his old age.

Since then, I have always made sure I have telephone numbers available to give to anyone in this situation or that I can use to get advice. I also have a range of agencies I can refer someone to or that I can contact for help. One of the most useful things the Church of England could do would be to ensure that every vicar has a handy reference guide with a range of phone numbers and web contacts to help them in this and any other kind of emergency, whether it be suicide, homelessness, mental health or some other kind of cry for help.

The most traumatic visit to the door started a process that was to last for months and got me embroiled in ethical issues that I had no idea I'd have to deal with as a vicar. Two hundred yards down the road, just inside the parish boundary, was the main pregnancy advisory clinic for East and West Sussex. The principal activity of a clinic like this is to advise and administer abortions, although they do provide education and other advice around contraception and birth planning. This is obviously a contentious subject and every Thursday a coalition of church groups would protest outside the clinic with banners decrying the work going on inside, accompanied by very explicit large-scale photographs about the horrors of this practice. I was aware of these protests but it didn't impact on my daily life until my doorbell rang one Thursday morning.

I opened the door to find two women, one of whom seemed very excited and asked if her friend could use my toilet. It turned out she was a protester and her 'friend' was a clinic client who had been to the clinic for an abortion and been given some medication and sent home to await the inevitable outcome. The protesters had persuaded her this was not a good idea and were looking for somewhere for her to make herself sick so that the medication would not be able to do its work. In that moment I had to decide what I thought about abortion, did I want to ally myself with these protesters, and how I should react to this extreme request. This was a lot to process on the spot. Fortunately, I could see that the 'friend' was already looking very reticent about this and was beginning to withdraw, so rather than answer the protester I spoke to her. She quickly confirmed that she was fine, she didn't need the toilet and just wanted to get home and immediately walked away, leaving me standing on the doorstep with a crestfallen protester.

Being confronted with this situation prompted me to do something about it. Whatever my thoughts were about the rights or wrongs of abortion, the fact is that this is legal in the UK and the clinic was providing perfectly legal help to women in distress. I felt that adding to that stress by protesting at the gates of the very organization that women were going to for help was not a particularly compassionate response. So I set to researching the issue and contacting the groups involved, asking them to come and see me for a chat.

It turned out that none of the churches involved in the protesting were from Brighton and in fact the response from the churches in this city was to set up a pregnancy counselling service themselves, providing a range of advice to anyone who unexpectedly found themselves pregnant. I managed to contact the various anti-abortion groups and invited them to come and see me so we could talk about the clinic. This resulted in two or three meetings, one of which included a powerpoint presentation from one of them linking their work to the abolition initiatives of William Wilberforce on slavery and Martin Luther King on racial discrimination. Another meeting became a kind of Pentecostal prayer meeting as people described God calling them to this mission and praying for me. My constant theme was irrespective of our views on abortion, where was the Christian compassion for women in distress, many of whom were coming to this clinic out of desperation. I tried to make the case to the protesters that their efforts should be directed to getting the law allowing abortion changed rather than penalizing the end users at the most awful time in their lives.

This began to escalate as others heard that I was researching this issue and showing an interest in it. Residents of the houses next door to the clinic started to get in touch because the protests were disruptive to them, other locals contacted me because they were concerned that the rights of women to choose were being affected, and before long I found myself collaborating with our local MP to organize a public meeting with the clinic to discuss this. This gave us a chance to hear from a range of people including the staff at the clinic who were feeling threatened by the protests while being fully aware that in the US some clinical staff had faced violence and death threats in the course of doing their work which they regarded as essential and caring.

The MP agreed to hold her regular weekly surgery in my church to understand further opinions from local residents as well as hearing about any other issues that were of concern in the area. I thought that was a reasonable thing to do until the day before the surgery was due to be held. Twenty-four hours before the meeting I started to be bombarded with extremely unpleasant emails from all over the country expressing displeasure that I would allow this 'babykiller' to use my church as a venue. It seemed that one of the protest groups was encouraging their supporters to contact me to try and dissuade me from allowing this meeting to go ahead and I had to endure a day of nasty messages that gave me some insight into the sort of abuse MPs receive for doing their jobs. Fortunately the surgery went off without any problems and a number of residents were able to air their views.

After this flurry of activity things began to calm down. The protesters either listened to my plea to target lawmakers and the government rather than the end-users of the clinic or they got fed up with standing outside in all weathers and the protests began to dwindle in size and frequency. Local residents were happier as there was less hassle on Thursday mornings and those who had been unable to sell their properties due to the turmoil found it easier to get buyers. I established a light touch relationship with the clinic and was able to offer my pastoral services to any staff who might need to talk to someone, and the clinic were happy to keep a stack of my business cards on hand for any clients who expressed some religious or spiritual concerns about abortion. Eventually protests stopped altogether apart from one or two nuns who would occasionally turn up to stand in silence outside the clinic and pray, something that they had always done and which felt to me to be the most appropriate Christian response. After some years of calm the clinic lost its contract with the NHS and vacated the building, which was recently bought by another organization who have set it up as a fertility clinic. I see something of God's divine action in this saga of a facility now dedicated to helping families create new life. The clinic has been redeemed for good, a modern day parable of God at work in our world.

Not every doorstep experience is so desperate or takes this long. There was the woman who used to come round once every three months or so asking for meat! There was never any conversation or chance to find out anything else from her as she just stood on the doorstep with two or three children in tow and would repeat 'We need some meat!'. There are various types of requests from visitors to the door, sometimes genuine and sometimes trying it on. I get frequent requests for money for the gas or electric meter and sometimes an unusual amount for a rail ticket to somewhere. That usually solicits an offer from me to go with those people to the train station to buy their ticket, an offer that is almost exclusively turned down.

One rainy night, in the middle of winter, the doorbell went and I opened up to find a very bedraggled man dressed in jeans and a rather large sweater which was sopping wet. We had a brief conversation about his lack of winter clothing and his need for money. My policy about money is generally not to give out any and this is based on advice from various workers with the homeless. In certain very limited circumstances I will give some cash, but I'm very clear to the recipient that it's a one-off donation to help them and there will be no further cash on any return visits. In this case, as it was his first time, I gave the guy some money and as he was soaked through, managed to find an old waterproof jacket of mine which I gave to him. A week later the same guy was back at the door, in the same kind of weather, wearing the same jeans and the same sopping wet jumper, but no jacket. Once I'd made it clear that I really meant what I'd said before about no more cash, I asked him why he wasn't wearing the jacket I'd given him previously in the pouring rain. He told me that he was cold a couple of nights ago so had burnt it to get warm! I wasn't sure whether to laugh because of the absurd idea that coats were more use as fuel or to cry because of such a desperate solution to need. I managed to find a second jacket to let him have and sent him on his way protected from the rain but cashless as previously promised.

Sometimes doorstep requests are unusual enough to make me pause and think of unusual solutions, like the Romanian guy who rang the doorbell and asked if he could have £48.50 for a ferry ticket. It seemed such a specific request that it felt genuine but I decided to stick to my policy and duly gave him £20 and blessed him on his way. Three days later the doorbell went again and it was the same guy with a similar request but this time he had walked the ten miles along the coast to Newhaven, spoken to the ferry ticket office and got them to give him a written note about the cost of a ticket to France. He then walked back to Brighton to see me and produced a slightly bedraggled note on official Newhaven Ferry paper confirming the cost of a one way ticket as £48.50 and showed me that he had kept the £20 I gave him before and managed to collect a further £20 from other donors. I was impressed with his perseverance and honesty and so gave him £10 to cover the rest of the ticket and my business card and asked if he would send me a postcard when he got back to Romania so that I knew what had happened to him. He went on his way with a brief thank you and I expected that I would never hear from him again.

Three months later, a postcard dropped onto the mat with a few words scrawled on the back and a Romanian stamp and postmark. The card simply said 'I'm home after a long walk, thank you'. I was overjoyed that my £30 donation and the determination of this man resulted in a reunion with his family and hopefully a new lease of life.

Some doorstep encounters can be quite serious, like the Saturday when I came home from a diocesan meeting to find two big guys lying on the grass in the vicarage front garden drinking tea and eating sandwiches. I said hello and went into the house to find out what was going on. While I was out my wife had answered the door to another request for help and as she knew I would be home soon had offered them some food and asked them to wait. I went out to talk with them and as I got nearer became aware of a really awful smell. I was used to the smell of homelessness but this was something different and after a few minutes of conversation one of the guys told me that they had stopped to ask for help as he was struggling to walk. He showed me a really nasty wound on his leg which turned out to be the source of the rotten smell. I am not a doctor but I did a para-medical degree at university and thought I knew what this was so I immediately called 999. An ambulance arrived pretty quickly and the paramedics soon confirmed that the wound was gangrenous and they needed to get the guy to hospital. While one of the medics dressed the man's leg and got them both transferred to the ambulance, I had a very bizarre conversation with the driver who announced that we'd met before because I'd married him! Once I got over the confusion of being married to an ambulance driver instead of my wife and realized that he meant I'd run the marriage service for him and his wife, the conversation turned to updates on his family and their lives since the wedding, interspersed with questions to the homeless guy about how he'd ended up getting injured and whether he was allergic to any medication. Eventually they were all bundled into the ambulance and headed off to hospital.

Incidents like this made us think about safety in the vicarage, especially when I'm not home. At the time we had three teenage children at home as well as my wife and we began to be a bit more cautious about opening the door and gave instructions to the children to never open the door if we weren't in the house. We now have a video doorbell fitted so that we can check who's at the door before opening it and I think it should be Church policy to have cameras on all vicarage front doors for the safety and security of their clergy. Interestingly, since we had this fitted, we've had a lot fewer random callers and I wonder if this acts as a bit of a deterrent.

Some doorstep visitors became quite familiar. There was the former soldier who would turn up in Brighton for four or five months every year and who we would see quite regularly. He would come to the door to have a chat or to tell me about some scrape he'd got into. Once or twice he asked if he could leave things with me for safe keeping. I was cautious about looking after a portable Bluetooth speaker for a couple of days but drew the line at a rucksack full of clothes and a large bottle of cider. He was always cheerful and ready with a joke and we would regularly see him in the street where he would loudly proclaim that my wife was far too gorgeous to be married to a vicar like me! For a while he started turning up at four o'clock in the morning and unsurprisingly I refused to open the door to him on those occasions and had a serious talk with him later about appropriate times to call.

One of the important things I try to maintain with all doorstep visitors is recognizing that they are human beings who are worthy of respect and dignity, irrespective of their circumstances. I always ask their names, give them mine, and attempt to have more of a conversation than 'can I have some money for the meter'. My wife would often come home to find me sat on the doorstep with someone while I listened to their life story. One of the greatest indignities for those who are homeless is that they are often not regarded as people but as problems to be solved or issues to be dealt with. At the heart of Christianity is the concept of incarnation, God becoming a human being, and that therefore there is divine value in every person, even if that person has a chaotic lifestyle or one that is different to ours. I always try to recognize the individual every time I'm approached for help, whether on the doorstep or by someone asking for money on the street. It's the greatest indignity to ignore fellow human beings and there's no harm in recognizing a person with a nod or a hello even if (and perhaps especially if) you're not able to give them any help.

Similarly, I believe that it's possible to have forthright, honest conversations with people about their situation in life and that they appreciate honesty and straight talking. Asking people in need about their journey through life and showing an interest in them is part of what it means to value someone, and being candid with them about their situation can open up helpful discussions about a positive way forward. This is especially true of so many ex-service personnel who end up on the streets after leading a life in the military where their lives have been totally ordered and provided for and who find it hard to cope in a society where nothing is handed to them and no-one is giving them any instructions on how to live.

Sometimes it's possible to provide real, practical help, especially if the doorstep request is for something achievable rather than cash for the meter. I got to know one of our callers who visited a few times over the course of three or four months. He was an example of someone who had ended up on the street after a succession of misfortunes that could have befallen any of us. He was made redundant, then his wife left him so he moved in with his mother. Sadly, she died and the landlord took back possession of their rented flat. This resulted in a period of depression, exacerbated by time spent living in hostels, and so eventually he decided to go on the road and found himself in Brighton with nothing but the rucksack on his back and a few quid in his pocket. I managed to help him find a room in a hotel that he could just about afford for a few weeks; he was able to come to the church for meals a couple of times a week and I gave him a list of other places he could get food. In the course of our conversations about his situation it became clear that he had family in another part of the country but he had felt too embarrassed about his situation to get in touch. It was a simple matter to let him use the church phone to call them and find out that they were worried about him, wanted to help and that he would be welcome with them. So I took him to the train station, bought him a ticket and waved him off to be reunited with his family; that was the last I ever saw of him.

Doorstep discoveries aren't always in the form of human beings and I find it odd what people think vicars might like or have a use for. We have a side door to our vicarage which opens onto a different street and for a whole year we regularly found a bag full of shopping hanging on the doorknob! I don't know whether someone thought the vicar needed a bit of help with shopping or whether these were intended for the foodbank, but that is where they ended up. Generous donations of shopping direct from the supermarket are better than the bags of half opened food we sometimes find by the door with a note saying that the donor is going away on holiday and thought we might be able to make good use of the contents of their fridge before they went off!

My most appreciated doorstep drop was coming home one day to find a large five-litre plastic water carrier embossed with an image of the Blessed Virgin Mary. This turned out to have come all the way from Lourdes and was full of holy water! As we're not the kind of church that uses holy water very often this has lasted for years! Many thanks to the anonymous donor for the years of blessing this wonderful gift has provided!

11

Religion and Politics

It is often said that religion and politics do not mix which puts me in a difficult spot as I get involved with both because I think Jesus got involved with both. If you care about your neighbours and the community they inhabit then sooner or later you are going to come across politics and politicians because they play such an important role in shaping the society around us. When you're involved in providing foodbanks and lunches, mental health and addiction support and assisting those who are homeless or in debt, you begin to realize that providing a sticking plaster to help those in need isn't enough and that at some point there needs to be some action on the root causes of these societal problems. As Dom Helder Camara said: 'When I feed the poor, they call me a saint, but when I ask why the poor are hungry, they call me a communist.' Addressing the needs of society inevitably leads to getting involved in politics and political debate.

Fairly early on in my time at St Luke's I found myself getting involved in local politics as I became a member, and then chair, of our local community association. The popularity of community associations can wax and wane with the tides of discontent in the neighbourhood. Nothing drives interest in a community organization like a dispute about a planning application, a proposal to change the parking arrangements or the closure of a much-loved pub. My community association baptism of fire started when I headed up selling off the church hall and continued with neighbourhood discussions about the local abortion clinic but it also spawned a number of more positive schemes.

Being a seaside city, we don't get much snow in Brighton but the first day of December in 2010 was unusual because we had a massive dump of snow across the whole city. It was a lovely start to the Advent season with the delights of snow days when schools were closed, people couldn't get to work and snowmen and women began appearing on the beach, but there were difficulties as well. St Luke's is on top of a hill and pretty much every road leading to the church is a steep uphill climb and the surrounding roads all have a gradient of some kind, some of them pretty severe. The main road past the church was gritted but then froze over, was gritted again adding another layer of ice to the already slick surface, and became impassable. Cars were being abandoned as they struggled to get up even the gentlest of inclines and some of the side roads became littered with cars at odd angles as people gave up trying to skate their way home and decided to walk. I remember walking through some local streets where a car had been discarded in the middle of a junction and watching it slowly slide sideways until it came to rest up against another deserted car which was only static because it was wedged against the pavement.

It was treacherous to walk anywhere and many streets became impassable. Some people were unable to leave their homes due to the icy conditions and there was a general spirit of neighbourliness and collaboration as people looked out for each other and offered to make trips to the shops for those who couldn't manage this. This situation only lasted for a few days but had a big effect on the local community and lived long in the memories of all of us because it became a great source of community cohesion.

Almost a year passed and the days grew shorter and the weather got colder and one of the community association committee members with a good memory asked how we were going to prepare for bad weather if it happened again. After some discussion it was decided that we should gather a list of potential volunteers and people who might need to be helped if this situation occurred again, so that the neighbourly assistance could be a little more co-ordinated next time. Co-ordination is great but it needs to have a co-ordinator! As everyone on the committee was a volunteer and I was the only one with free access to a photocopier, a relatively neutral email address and had some

RELIGION AND POLITICS

legitimacy as a community organizer, I found myself as the de facto point of contact for the Big Freeze project.

We created a questionnaire explaining the idea behind the scheme, asking people if they thought they might need help in a severe weather crisis and also asking if people willing to volunteer would give their contact details. The church photocopier worked overtime printing 2,000 questionnaires and a small team of volunteers and church folk undertook to leaflet every house in the area. Pretty soon completed survey forms began to drop into the church letterbox and before long I had a list of 70 or so volunteers and half a dozen households who thought they might need help if the snow came. At the same time I contacted the council, who were happy to supply 20 snow shovels and half a dozen street brooms but couldn't do anything about setting up street bins for grit, so I went out and bought half a dozen sacks of gritting salt. All of this got stored in the church cellar ready for the next snowfall and the opportunity to call everyone out.

In the 13 years since this was set up I have activated the scheme once! Climate change seems to be doing our job for us and winters are becoming warmer and wetter and we have not had any significant snow in Brighton for at least ten years. What I do have as a result of this is an amazing list of volunteers who have been called on at other times, especially during the pandemic. The church also established itself as a hub for the community, and the goodwill and positive PR from setting up this scheme has helped enormously to generate an affirmative attitude towards us and church in general. Although I didn't know it, this was my first foray into community organizing, a process exemplified by Citizens UK, something which became a much bigger part of my life later on. It was also my first example of how local councils can be helpful and contribute to the betterment of their residents if approached in the right way with a simple, achievable objective.

Politics both local and national reared its head a few years later when the country went to the polls for a referendum on our involvement with Europe. As the campaigns for and against being part of Europe hotted up, the community association was very concerned about the possibility of discord in the neighbourhood as the different sides of the argument were debated in pubs and cafes and any other chatty forum, including online discourse. The committee were universally in favour of remaining in Europe but thought it would be a good idea to provide an opportunity for people to chat about the upcoming referendum in a non-threatening, neutral space where all views were welcome.

There had been a tradition of holding a summer barbecue in June which was usually organized by the church in a local park, although attendance in recent years had been pretty poor and mostly consisted of the church congregation, the committee members and a few local families. As we discussed how we might engage more people, the idea of a street party was floated and seemed like a really good way to get people chatting to each other in a convivial atmosphere, especially as it would be just outside the front door of those who lived in the street that was hosting the event. To add a hint that the event was intended to help people talk about the referendum, we decided that it would be a Europe themed party with food provided by the Real Junk Food Project and everyone invited to bring a European dessert to share with others. A Sunday early in June was set for the event and work started on all the admin and publicity.

In hindsight the advertising for the event was a little one-sided. Posters were European Community blue with yellow wording and a circle of yellow stars remarkably reminiscent of the European flag prominent in the middle of the design. At the last minute a header of multicoloured bunting was added to try and mitigate the overwhelming emphasis on Europe, but this didn't fool anyone into thinking that Brexiteers were just as welcome as Europhiles. A couple of committee members got on with arranging a street closure with the council and our local councillors were invited along with our local MP, all of whom were known to be supporters of staying in Europe.

The day of the street party dawned hot and sunny and once we'd finished our morning service the congregation were press-ganged into carrying tables and chairs round to the designated street which was already festooned with bunting and closed off with signs to stop any traffic. There then followed a really happy afternoon as young and old, neighbours and friends got to know each other over vegetarian curry and a bewildering variety of desserts from trifle to baklava, sponge cake to tiramisu. I don't think there was much talk about the referendum except perhaps with the politicians who I suspect were quite keen to avoid the subject anyway. But what started that day was a wonderful tradition.

Less than two weeks after that first street party, tragically, the MP Jo Cox was murdered by a far-right sympathizer as she was about to hold a meeting in her Yorkshire constituency. In the aftermath of this terrible event her husband set up a number of initiatives in her memory, one of which was the 'Great Get Together', an annual celebration of everything that unites communities. As this was exactly what we were trying to achieve with our street party, this then became the theme for the following year. Since then, the event has grown in popularity with three local streets being partially closed and a whole programme of events being organized including local bands, Morris Dancers, children's activities and a dog show. As it is still happening on a Sunday, I suggested to the organizing committee that we start the day by holding our church service in the street, an idea that was enthusiastically embraced by all involved. So now there is always a Sunday in June when we go walkabout to the local street and residents and neighbours who never come anywhere near the church get to watch us from their front doors, and sometimes even join in, as we worship, pray and share communion in the heart of our community.

Closing streets for a street party is no mean feat in this city where parking and traffic routinely top the list of conversation topics. It seems that there is always someone who is unhappy with the number of cars on their street, either stationary or passing through, and woe betide anyone who tries to do something about this. Over the years I have been here there have been a number of proposals for campaigns to turn one street or another into a play street or to introduce a one-way system or some form of traffic calming to slow vehicles down and make things safer.

One local issue that everyone agreed with though was the shocking state of Pigeon Poo Bridge.

Pigeon Poo Bridge is a local intersection just down the hill from the church where a couple of major roads run under the main railway lines from Brighton to London. As this is close to the station there are a lot of lines and the bridges running under them are linked, forming a 100m tunnel containing three or four lanes of traffic going in and out of the city. It's dark and dank and covered in graffiti and, in theory, was shrouded in netting to prevent birds roosting or nesting on the ledges and girders that were part of the structure. The problem was that the netting was well past its sell-by date and full of more holes than it was supposed to have, and so hundreds of pigeons were able to get inside and use the underside of these bridges as their home. The whole cycle of pigeon life was represented here, with nests holding eggs which then hatched, fledglings falling out of their home to be run over on the road, adult pigeons feeding, breeding and excreting everywhere and a fair few of them dying, decaying and dropping to the ground once the netting gave way to release them to gravity.

It was awful and some residents informed me that they wanted to do something about this. They had arranged to meet a reporter from the local paper to highlight this eyesore and asked if I would come along. The next day I headed down to meet them and as I approached the little gang that were already talking about the problem and taking photos, I felt something wet drop on my head. Yes, on my way to talk to a newspaper about pigeon poo bridge I had been pooed on, a perfect photo opportunity to start the campaign off! We got a nice splash in the newspaper but that didn't make any difference to the situation. To get anything done about a problem like this requires real persistence and a lot of hard research because it turns out all the constituent parts of a structure like this are managed by different people.

The council has responsibility for the highway, which includes the pavements and the road and any street furniture such as street lights or traffic lights; but the walls and roof and the structure of the bridge are the responsibility of the owners, in this case Network Rail. They own and manage 30,000 bridges, tunnels and viaducts and so receiving a complaint about the state of one of them from a local vicar hardly registers with them. After months of fruitless attempts to get a response from them we, or to be more exact my wife, decided to get political. We called a public meeting at the bridge with our local MP as a way of shaming Network Rail to respond and to our amazement they turned up. Even more amazingly they told us they were going to do something about it and so we waited with bated breath to see what would happen.

Eventually contractors moved in and over the course of a fortnight all the old bird netting was removed and new netting installed across the whole site. The contractors left satisfied that the problem was solved and the council sent round a team of street cleaners with pressure washers to tidy up the pavements. Unfortunately, this wasn't the end of the story because the new netting was rubbish and the wily pigeons very quickly found their way inside the netting to their usual perches. While getting in was easy, getting out was not and so within a couple of weeks the nets were full of the bodies of dead pigeons, rotting and dropping bits of bird onto the pedestrians below. As the self-appointed monitor of this project, I made regular trips down the road to see what was going on and at one point counted more than 30 dead birds hanging above our heads, not exactly the solution we had hoped for. I took another walk down with a local resident who was a photographer so that we could document this disaster which was not only bad for pedestrians but also cruel to the birds. It was an advantage that our MP was the only Green party politician in Parliament because she was copied in on our next set of communications with Network Rail which included the threat of legal action under the Wildlife and Countryside Act 1981.

A few weeks later the contractors started all over again, this time being more thorough in their work and additionally installing one way exits from the netting so that any errant birds who did find their way into the forbidden zone also had a means of escape. Once again, the pavements were jet washed and we decided to celebrate this community victory by commissioning an artwork, thanks to some public art funding we'd been directed to by the MP. After a short consultation and some community workshops held in the church, a local artist, assisted by groups of local families, set to work on a pixellated artwork of flowers and greenery by painting the bricks of the bridge like a massive painting by numbers picture on the side of the bridge. Not only did this add some colour to the dingy landscape of the bridge, it also discouraged graffiti artists from adding their own designs which the council had also kindly removed from the walls.

Alliances between the church and local and national politicians can produce results that benefit the whole community but it's also necessary for faith communities to keep a healthy distance from politicians because it's important for us to be able to challenge and question policies that we see are causing harm or distress. Helping to set up a local chapter of Citizens UK here in Brighton has been transformational in this, because we have combined with other faith and non-faith organizations to campaign for better wages for care workers, mental health counsellors in schools and improved local public transport provision. This is part of our mission to be a force for good in our local community, listening to their concerns and bringing them to the attention of those who have the power to make change.

12

Serving God and Mammon

Once a year, in November, I sign a declaration about my own beliefs and our church practice during the previous twelve months which generates us a small grant that helps to keep us solvent as a church. This declaration confirms my adherence to the *'Protestant and Evangelical principles of the Church of England'* and my *'cordial attachment'* to the institution, that I accept the 39 Articles of Religion, that I have not referred to the table at the east end of the church as anything other than a holy table, and I have not put a cross, crucifix, lights, candlesticks or flowers on it. In addition, I have to confirm that I have not celebrated the Eucharist in the eastward facing position and that I reject the practice of *'auricular confession'* and will not allow it to be practised in the parish. Once I've signed this declaration and submitted it to the diocese, we receive a small grant from the Newmarch Trust which is a result of the interest accrued on a fund set up in 1912. Major-General Newmarch was concerned about the popularity of the Oxford movement in Brighton and the fact that a number of churches had been built specifically to foster catholic practice in this city and so put aside a sum of money to encourage evangelical habits in opposition to these papist traditions. This forms a small part of the financial landscape of this church that I serve and to a certain extent am responsible for.

One of the many things that theological college doesn't teach you about is finance, which is ironic as I turned up to train to be a vicar with nothing but an overdraft to my name. There is a reticence to talk about money in Anglican churches in the UK, unlike some of our American cousins who seem perfectly happy to hold the collection plate under the noses of their congregations while preachers fly around in private jets, drive gold-plated Rolls Royces and live in massive mansions. In contrast folk in the Church of England seem embarrassed that we have to ask people for a donation when they come to church, and those sat in the pews seem to think that putting £2 in the collection every week is more than enough to save their souls, pay the vicar and stop the church falling down.

One of the difficulties for the Church of England is that the general public think of it as a very rich organization with enormous assets, which is all centrally funded and therefore doesn't need local folk to put their hands in their pockets. To a certain extent that is not far from the truth as clearly the Church of England is very rich on paper. It owns a massive portfolio of property spread all over the country in the form of church buildings, parish halls, parsonages, churchyards and glebe land. It also has significant investments that are used to create income for church projects and cover central expenditure, and the Church Commissioners have done a great job in recent years in earning a better than average return on these investments and contributing the income received towards church projects. They manage to do all this while also being a significant ethical investor.

But at parish level the picture is much less rosy and is often extremely difficult. Each parish church is expected to fund the running costs of their own church buildings, to pay the expenses of their vicar and to contribute to central resources by paying a contribution to the diocese of which they are a part. I have mentioned that the finances of St Luke's as portrayed in the parish profile looked very healthy and hinted there that this looked a bit too good to be true. The parish profile given to me before I started the job contained a summary of the accounts but as I took office in May I didn't get to see any actual accounts until early the following year as we began to prepare for our Annual Parochial Church Meeting (APCM). The APCM is effectively the AGM that every church has to hold once a year and which has to take place in the first quarter of the year before 31st May. Before that I occasionally got to see bank statements that seemed to be positive but didn't hold a great deal of money and we received a finance report at every PCC meeting, but looking back at the minutes I realize that these were mostly about signatories for the bank and hardly any summary of our actual cash! I knew that we had £30,000 or £40,000 in the bank and assumed that all the other money I'd seen in the summary was held in a deposit account or invested somewhere.

So, it wasn't until I'd been in post for nearly nine months that I saw a draft set of accounts and realized we were in big trouble! It turned out that what I thought was a significant reserve of cash did not exist because one of the items listed in our accounts under 'funds' was the church hall. This dilapidated old liability of a building was listed in our accounts as part of our funds carried forward each year and so was not cash at all. What was worse was that the figure in the accounts was a valuation that was a bit suspect because it was based on insurance value which was way above the actual sale value we managed to achieve when we eventually sold it in 2012 (see Chapter 3). This left a hole in what I had understood to be our accounts of more than £400,000, so rather than having hundreds of thousands of pounds in a reserve bank account somewhere, we were actually spending approximately £20,000 per year more than we were receiving and the quite small amount of cash in the bank account was dwindling rapidly.

I instigated a series of discussions with the PCC about this and we decided to hold a gift day to ask the congregation to focus on giving and I also began the process of cutting our costs by reducing some of the part-time staff that were doing various admin jobs in the church. Having previously run my own business and before that being a production manager responsible for budgeting major TV projects, I was used to keeping an eye on finances and familiar with the idea of a 'run rate' as a way of monitoring how an operation was doing financially. Knowing that our income fell short of our regular expenditure by £1,600 per month gave us all a nice easy target figure as we tried to remedy the situation, as well as an idea of when we would hit rock bottom if we didn't do something about this.

A significant proportion of this expenditure is the parish share, which is also known as the parochial contribution to the diocesan common fund. This is the donation the parish is asked to make towards the running costs of the Church of England to cover the stipend of their vicar, central diocesan services and staff, training of curates, pensions and national Church costs and is calculated in different ways by different dioceses. The diocese in which I work levies it as a flat rate according to the level of staffing of each parish, so there is a standard level of contribution defined if you have a full-time vicar, a lower one for a half-time priest and lower again for a house for duty (house for duty is when a priest lives in the vicarage in return for running the church on a part-time basis but receives no stipend). Others use a formula that takes into account the deprivation index of the parish or the number on the electoral roll and some dioceses set a suggested level of payment but leave it up to the individual parishes to contribute what they feel they can afford. Whatever the system, it's very hard to view this payment as anything other than a tax for being a Church of England church and even harder to explain this to the congregation when they are being asked to pay more than three times the vicars' stipend into a central fund without seeing much in return. When trying to explain this to people outside the church I refer to it as our licence fee for being able to call ourselves a Church of England church.

This is particularly difficult when congregations are also responsible for paying for the costs of the church building, despite this not being owned by them. So the congregation of St Luke's has to pay the utility bills, council tax and all maintenance and repairs for a building that most of them only use once a week and which is owned by the Church of England. This also includes structural expenses such as fixing church spires or organs, maintaining precious ancient murals, memorials and statues and looking after the drains and any other potentially ruinous expenses and is the reason behind the old tradition of a giant funding thermometer positioned outside a church to show the progress of their latest campaign to raise money for a particular restoration project. In addition, the PCC is expected to pay my council tax and expenses as well as any decorative expenses for the vicarage, although at least the diocese pays for the structural upkeep of the house. This is a significant financial burden for people who are giving out of their own generosity and because of their Christian faith. In our diocese the contribution asked for each year usually equates to 100% of our income, which would leave us no money to pay for the electric, buy food for our various food projects or cover any repair or maintenance bills. Consequently, we pay what we can, always aware that this may not be viewed favourably by those who make decisions about resourcing this church, especially when it comes to appointing the next vicar.

There is also an unspoken connection between finance and faith, although recently this has been much more explicit due to the wider Church discussions about sexuality, with whole churches choosing to not pay their parish share or paying it into a separate fund rather than their diocese. I experienced this in a much more personal way early on in my time in this parish as it became increasingly clear that I was on a different page to some members of the congregation on certain things. Slowly over the first two or three years of my incumbency people began to leave, taking their money with them. Some just drifted away, others were more explicit and emailed me to let me know that they were concerned about the direction the church was going in and felt God was telling them to leave. Often these were good evangelical folk who had been schooled in the concept of tithing and therefore gave 10 per cent of their significant income to the church. There's a great temptation to give in when you see a family leaving church and £1,500 a month disappearing from the collection plate because we've had what I perceive to be a minor disagreement about a point of church order or doctrine. But ultimately I feel I have to stick to my principles and try to respond graciously to everyone who chooses to take this line.

I feel that the kind of inclusivity I see modelled by God welcomes everyone, whether we hold the same views or not. I value my sisters and brothers in Christ whatever their view on sexuality, atonement, priesthood, the sacraments and a whole raft of other topics, because I am united with them as fellow children of God with Jesus our brother. Whether we like it or not we are part of the family of God because of Jesus' birth, death and resurrection and just like any family we will always have disagreements but we still have a blood connection that is permanent and eternal. I long for a church where people feel they can disagree with me (as long as they do it politely and graciously), because striving together makes us better people and deepens our understanding of what it means to be Christian.

The vast majority of those who have decided over the years to leave the church I serve have not left church but simply transferred to another one, which I see as a form of church planting and am grateful that their gifts and their money are now benefitting someone else. The irony of this is that they usually move to a church that is already well resourced, not just through the giving of their congregation but also because of a programme of centralized Church of England funding. In 2014 the Archbishops Council set up the Strategic Development Fund, allocating £198 million to be distributed over six years to churches for mission projects. In Brighton and Hove the vast majority of funding received through this initiative was given to churches following a model developed by Holy Trinity Brompton (HTB) in London.

I sometimes describe St Luke's style and ethos before my arrival as being HTB Lite. The church was the only Anglican congregation in central Brighton that had a worship band, used contemporary songs with lyrics on projector screens, and had an informal approach to Sunday mornings and occasional evening services for young people. It was also a home of the Alpha course and had an emphasis on the inspiration of the Holy Spirit as an important part of Christian faith. Just prior to my licensing as priest-in-charge, a city centre church just a mile down the road became the first major church plant outside London for the real HTB experience. This was a natural draw for some of the congregation of St Luke's who saw a much more professional set up with internationally renowned worship leaders such as Matt Redman and Martin Smith 'performing' regularly on Sunday mornings and a glossy London clientele who had all committed to moving to the south coast to support this exciting initiative and help transform the second most Godless city in the country (as described in the church attendance numbers in the 2011 census statistics).

Over the years since then, this enterprise has received millions of pounds of SDF money and has planted or revitalized half a dozen congregations across the city. The money has been used to employ youth workers, worship leaders, operation managers, associate priests and people in a variety of pastoral roles and there has been a proliferation of this style of church in a landscape that was previously dominated by high church tradition. Congregations have grown and there are significantly more young people involved in church in this city than there were before and this is to be celebrated as a good thing. This 'resource church' model has been replicated across the country; it has now become a commonplace strategic model for dioceses to follow and is often funded from central Church of England coffers.

But this focus on resourcing one church with additional funds and people has a knock-on effect for those not part of that project. St Luke's has lost congregation members to this initiative, along with their financial contribution to the life of this church as well as the loss of their talent and energy. Often this loss has been concentrated on a younger demographic so that we have also lost something of the generational mix that makes church congregations so unique. The money invested by the central Church of England has not created a resource for the whole church landscape in this city, but has fostered an imbalance of haves and have nots which causes some resentment in those of us who struggle to cover our costs let alone fund mission initiatives that could benefit the church in our locality. It's also a misnomer to describe these as resource churches because the resources they have are only shared with churches in their own family. I have asked if we could share in some of the riches of their worship talent by borrowing someone occasionally to help our church services but have always been told that no-one is available, so we continue to struggle with backing tracks and hymns on video while down the road I know there are teams of musicians sat in the pews waiting for their turn on a rota to lead worship once a month. Similarly with youth and children's work, volunteers to feed the homeless and all the ancillary skills needed to run a church such as bookkeepers, building managers and fundraisers. I've even been told that the resource church can't publicize a mission event we were running because they only allow publicity about their own events to be placed in their church. I can't help feeling that £5m spread around 15 different churches with different approaches to mission might have produced a greater variety in types of church growth than giving it all to one flavour of church.

Of course, I understand that national Church finances are tight, I see that every time that I look at our own church bank account. In the face of declining congregations, the rising cost of living and the difficulty of managing a huge federated institution like the Church, choices have to be made about where to put money and what to encourage, and the corollary of that is that some churches will decline and that hard decisions need to be taken about allocation of resources, both financial and human. All I experience on the frontline of church ministry is the constant stress of managing the books when sometimes the church bank account is only a few thousand pounds away from an overdraft. While I was familiar with owing the bank money when I was young, I don't want the church to be in that same position and I don't think it's a responsible way for a faith organization to behave. I'm grateful for people like Major-General Newmarch who through their foresight continue to help some of us in these difficult times.

13

Happily Ever After

So what does it look like to have a happy church, without the clappy label that is sometimes still attributed to us at St Luke's, and is being a happy church a good thing?

In many ways the church I serve now is a lot easier without the arguments, the stresses of things going wrong, the projects that seem like a good idea initially but turn out to be fraught with problems and the disagreements over anything from doctrine to the type of cups we use for coffee after church. Are we stable as a congregation? Not at all. There are still stresses around finance, mental health, safeguarding, buildings, demographics and numbers. There are still things that wake me up at four in the morning and drive me to my desk to draft emails which then sit in my pending folder until they can be sent at a reasonable time of day so that no-one realizes I'm working in the hours of darkness before the dawn.

One of the things I struggle with is the urge to always try for perfection. This rears its head in relation to what I used to describe as the Sunday morning shop window. I always want our main Sunday morning service to be slick and interesting with good content for the regulars and a warm welcome for any visitors so that they feel comfortable and included and interested to find out more. As the main time that we get together as a community of faith I have very high expectations for our weekly gathering. I want it to be full of inspiring worship, I expect people to be moved in prayer, to show concern for the world and to meet God in the sacraments. I aim to engage everyone for a full hour whether they're seven or seventy with thoughtful teaching for all ages that will help them in their Christian journey whether they're in church for the first time or have been coming for their whole life. Sunday mornings should include worship, prayer, discipleship, fellowship, encounter with God, peace with each other and lessons for life that will stand us in good stead for the coming week. It's no wonder that in attempting to do all these things we often fail to do any of them well.

I was drawn up short one day when talking about our Sunday services with the PCC and bemoaning the fact that everything rested on my shoulders and that it was very hard to delegate responsibility for these as the PCC were often asking me to. One of the committee was a builder, and after pointing out that I found it hard to delegate because I was too much of a perfectionist he then directed us to consider what the Bible says about building. Psalm 118, Matthew 21, Mark 12, Luke 20 and Acts 4 all talk about a stone that is rejected by the builders becoming a cornerstone. Cornerstones are part of the foundation of a building upon which everything else is based and if a stone is rejected it's because its imperfect or flawed. So when the Bible talks about an imperfect stone becoming a cornerstone it's saying that it's OK to be lacking in some way and that God uses what is unsatisfactory and deficient to build the church. In fact, as we are all imperfect human beings it's a given that everything we do will be inadequate and unsatisfactory because that's part of what it means to be human. The consequence of that is that I should stop worrying about making everything perfect on a Sunday morning and let God work despite my imperfections.

This really struck home for me and is something about which I constantly remind myself. It doesn't stop me still wanting every Sunday service to be the absolute epitome of perfection so that every person leaves the church at the end of the morning inspired and joyful, praising God for meeting with them and determined to put their faith into practice in a new way from now on. I have slowly come to realize that it is not the shop window for strangers that I thought it was and that the individual encounters I and others have with people during the week are far more important in spreading the good news of Jesus to those around us, especially given our St Francis-inspired informal tagline of 'preach the gospel at all times, and when necessary use words'.

I've started to say that Sundays are almost the least important thing that we do compared to all the work that goes on midweek to help those in need. In many ways Monday to Saturday is our shop window, the place where people get to experience the love of God in the social welfare projects we provide and Sunday mornings should be a kind of staff meeting where all the shop workers gather to be refreshed and inspired for the work of the week. That's a model of church that seems to me to be close to what we see going on in the New Testament as the early church met together to build each other up in worship so that they were able to go about the work of helping the poor and the widows during the week. Sundays were about topping up the spiritual engines of those early Christians for the work of preaching the gospel both in words and actions.

So is being a happy church a good thing? I think not. I think church folk should always be discontented at the way the world is as long as there is injustice, inequality, poverty and discontent around. As long as we're aware that God's kingdom has not come on earth as it is in heaven, that there are those who do not have enough daily bread, that evil continues to roam our streets and that forgiveness is a hard thing to come by. I don't want church to be a refuge from the realities of life or an escape from day-to-day drudgery. I want church to be real about the world we live in, real about the failings in all of us, and galvanized to try and do something to make things better. I want the church to stop obsessing about sex and put all that energy into eradicating foodbanks, fighting for affordable housing, providing pastoral care for the isolated and helping those with mental health needs.

Nationally I want the church to invest in serving their local communities by finding out what their concerns are and helping to address those concerns in the most appropriate way possible. I believe that when people see the church listening to them and helping them then it will grow because they will see that church has a purpose and that faith is relevant. This will be evident not because we've invested in making our buildings glossier and filling them with high tech PA systems and flat screen TVs or setting them up like musty museums full of ancient artifacts and old traditions, but because they are filled with the living God who loves and cares for them.

I am passionate about this way of living out the Christian faith. A faith that wraps an apron around my waist and summons me to my knees in service of those around me in solidarity with Jesus who did this for his friends and bids us to do the same. This is what it means to be a Real Life Rev.